Retiring Spain

Cyril Holbrook

AGE Concern

BOOKS

©2004 Cyril Holbrook
Published by Age Concern England
1268 London Road
London SW16 4ER

First published 2004

Editor Richenda Milton-Thompson
Production Vinnette Marshall
Design and typesetting GreenGate Publishing Services
Printed in Great Britain by Bell & Bain Ltd, Glasgow

A catalogue record for this book is available from the British Library.

ISBN 0-86242-385-6

Every effort has been taken to ensure the accuracy of the information contained in *Retiring to Spain*, but Age Concern England and the author cannot accept any responsibility for any errors that may exist, or for changes that occur after publication.

DEDICATION

A few chapters further along in the Old Testament from the Ten Commandments Moses spells out how foreigners should be treated. He instructs:

And if a stranger sojourn with thee in your land, ye shall not vex him. But the stranger that dwelleth with you shall be unto you as one born among you, and thou shalt love him as thyself.

This book is dedicated to the many Spaniards who do just that, not because they feel that in so doing they are obeying a commandment passed on from the Almighty, but because they are naturally friendly people. Of course, not all the Spanish treat the expatriates living among them as themselves. Indeed, there are some who, considering themselves in a position of authority, seem to enjoy taking any opportunity to vex the stranger. But in spite of the obstacles to understanding presented by the language barrier and their different approaches to life, foreigners are usually greeted with a warmth other than that from the Iberian sun, which is not often encountered elsewhere.

My fellow strangers who have shown the determination and flexibility necessary to settle in what can still be a strange land should also take a bow. By offering advice and help, and sometimes through their naiveté, they have provided much of the material for this book which will hopefully guide others along the path they have already trodden. Among them, special mention must be made of the folk who help the expat community through Age Concern España and who provided valuable input to this volume. Thank you all. All of them, *españoles* and *extranjeros* from many lands, know who they are without a roll call from which somebody who has been a boon would be bound to be missed.

In England thanks are due to Age Concern publisher, Richard Holloway, who co-ordinated the whole project, and thanks to whom I was fortunate to have Richenda Milton-Thompson as editor for it was her literary midwifery that ensured a safe delivery after prolonged gestation.

Cyril Holbrook

CONTENTS

ABOUT THE AUTHOR

Cyril Holbrook moved to Spain with his wife and son in 1986 after a successful career in journalism in the UK. Though varied before, his range of professional activity has been much wider since.

Born into a chapel-going family in the Cambridgeshire Fens, Cyril was educated at March Grammar School. He joined *The Cambridgeshire Times* series of local newspapers as a reporter and completed his training after serving at the Central Fighter Establishment of the Royal Air Force during his National Service.

He moved to Bristol as a sub-editor on the *Western Daily Press* before returning to East Anglia in a similar capacity on the *Eastern Evening News* in Norwich. In 1967 he took over the Cromer office, covering North Norfolk for the *Eastern Evening News* and *Eastern Daily Press* as well as the local weekly.

After 12 years in Norfolk, Cyril joined the *Evening Telegraph* in Peterborough as deputy chief sub-editor before being invited to become production editor on *Angling Times*, the world's biggest angling newspaper, which was also owned by East Midland Allied Press. In 1976 he was appointed editor of *Tackle & Guns*, the trade magazine devoted to the sports of fishing and shooting, a position he held for 10 years.

During that time, he and his wife Anne – whom he married in 1959 – came to know the Costa del Sol and bought a holiday home in Benalmádena. Their decision to move to Andalucía permanently with their son has led to Cyril working on several newspapers, magazines and radio stations serving the English-speaking population in southern Spain. After writing a book about his angling experiences – *Fishing From My Angle*, which was published by David & Charles in 1988 – he edited a magazine based on satellite TV programmes and sold advertisements for the local Spanish newspaper's English supplement. He was also consultant at the launch of a successful monthly glossy, edited a golf magazine (though he has never played a round in his life), was assistant-editor on a Sunday paper and has written for several publications and assisted others in editorial capacities.

He also provided material for a guidebook on Spain and has handled publicity for enterprises as diverse as a new golf course, an Australian singer and a banger-racing circuit. For three years he worked with the local mayor to further the interests of the large number of foreign residents in the area, running a radio programme to help them integrate into the community. He still translates brochures and booklets into English for the town hall from time to time, as well as contributing articles to the local press. Cyril and his wife spend part of each summer in the Fens where his mother is thriving in her nineties.

INTRODUCTION

A survey carried out for a national newspaper in the United Kingdom in 2002, revealed the surprising statistic that more than half
those polled would like to live abroad. A whole basket of reasons
was given, from the climate and over-taxation, to house prices and
the number of foreigners living in Britain. This latter might appear an
odd comment in view of the fact that those making it were saying
they would like to become foreigners themselves.

The stumbling block preventing many from doing anything about
fulfilling their dream is the necessity of earning a living. Of course,
there are those who overcome this hurdle by working overseas,
often with the intention of returning home once their tour of duty
abroad is over. However, once freed from this shackle due to having
a sufficient income to live on without working – usually thanks to an
early pension or the arrival of the official retirement birthday – thousands do make the momentous move and head for the sun, not as
a temporary measure but to make another country their home.

Because it has been the favourite holiday destination for people
from Britain for decades, Spain is the recipient of much of this extra
wealth and experience. Living there, however, is an entirely different
thing from being one of the millions of tourists who visit the country
each year. Enjoying what a resort has to offer may be wonderful for
a fortnight, but would you get bored after a few months? Making
your travellers' cheques last a week or two may be fine, but how
about making your savings last the rest of your life?

If you are one of those who have cherished the dream of getting
away from the greyness and into the sunshine – or simply wondered
what it would be like to be an expatriate – here is a book which will
help you avoid many of the pitfalls.

The author deliberately says 'many' and not 'all' because he knows from a quarter of a century of personal experiences, as well as those of friends and acquaintances who have served an even longer apprenticeship as Hispanophiles, that nobody knows them all. Anyone who thinks they do will surely blunder into another hole they could never even have imagined was there.

Where the word 'all' does apply is to every bit of legal advice offered. The information has been carefully researched and made as current and valid as possible. However, in these days of coming to terms with the requirements of a United Europe as well as those of a rapidly evolving society, anything designed to protect the expatriate is of necessity founded on shifting sands rather than solid rock. The information contained in these pages will, however, help make the transition to a sunny and healthy retirement a reality.

The stories of the calamities which have befallen those who have set out to make a new life for themselves and their families in Spain are all authentic. Brought together as they are, and recounted in short order, there is a tendency for the overall impression to be one of enormous difficulties to be overcome. It must be remembered, however, that they are culled from the experiences of many people over a period of 20 years or so. Don't let them put you off. They are only repeated here – with the names changed to protect the innocent and to avoid embarrassment – as warnings of what *can* happen. It should not be thought for a moment that any of them *will* befall you. Indeed, isn't it true that being made aware of an obstacle on any path is the best way of ensuring you do not trip over it? That is the spirit in which they are included within these covers, not to scare but to shed light on the route you may wish to follow.

1 Pros and cons

The climate

The biggest single reason for most people deciding to retire to Spain has to be the weather. Other considerations obviously come into the picture but if, for example, Málaga had Bergen's rain and Bergen had the Costa del Sol's sunshine, Britons would be planning to go and live in Norway instead.

Ever since schooldays, when geography teachers attempted to make young minds grasp that a Mediterranean climate meant hot, dry summers and mild, wet winters, reliable summers have been the envy of those in less fortunate lands. Generations of northern Europeans who spend time sheltering in the pavilion instead of being out on the playing field and whose every scheduled event carries the proviso 'If wet, in the village hall', have dreamt of knowing that it will be fine tomorrow.

In parts of Spain you can bank on outdoor activities being sure of sunshine from April to September, and the rest of the year is as likely to provide shirt-sleeve weather as an English summer. It is to these areas, rather than the less fortunate parts of the Iberian Peninsular, that the majority of expatriates head. The contrary side of this is that there can be just too much sunshine in July and August. Even holidaymakers, who cover themselves with lotion against sunburn in a determined bid to return home with as deep a tan as possible, can be forced from the beach in the middle of the day. Local folk who have grown up with these temperatures automatically seek the shade … and so do expatriates, once they get used to the idea that they don't have to spend every minute outside. After all, it's going to be fine again tomorrow.

Then the siesta makes sense, and you don't care if shops shut from lunchtime till 5 or 6pm because you are not going to stir outside during the afternoon anyway. Eating late begins to seem reasonable as well. Evenings are not chilly and you can sit outdoors until late if you like, so who wants to eat when it's 40° in the shade, let alone cook. So the temperature really forges a different lifestyle, a more open-air, leisurely lifestyle, which is often quoted as another main reason for heading south.

Traditionally, many expatriates return to their homeland to spend at least part of the summer with friends or family, though the coming of air conditioning has made homes along the Spanish coast more comfortable when it gets *seriously* hot. Winter is the time when the climate is appreciated most. There are rainy days, really rainy days, when torrents turn roads into rivers. But unless you head into the hills, you are never likely to feel a frost. On January afternoons in parts of the South, the temperature can hit 30° Celsius on a sunny terrace. That is when anything on the downside of life in Spain can be put into perspective simply by listening to the British weather forecast or tuning into the news and watching the havoc being wreaked by the elements where you would have been had you not moved to Spain.

Things can be different on the Spanish islands with less predictable precipitation in the Canaries and rather cooler winters in the Balearics, despite their Mediterranean setting. The Atlantic islands are famed for their all-year-round temperature stability, but for the lack of the cooking summer of the mainland you have to put up with prevalent winds. And, of course, if you choose to live in Galicia or on the Bay of Biscay in the north, the climate is more like Cornwall than Cartagena.

Savings

The climate brings considerable savings too. In the warmer South, heating bills can be minimal, and even in the cooler parts of the country they are likely to be considerably less than in the UK. In some areas, there will be few days when any form of heating is required, even during the cooler months, except in the evenings or when the household is sitting around. Logs are always available for an open fire if you want one, and the advent of air conditioning has helped in this direction too. Most systems have a heating element as well and this can boost the temperature in winter instead of cooling it in summer.

Wills and property taxes

One immediate item on the debit side if you decide to live in Spain or own a property there is the necessity of making another will. A Spanish will is not obligatory, but it is highly recommended that you make one if you have anything of value in the country. While it is possible to make provision for most things to be protected from inheritance tax, a flat or house is going to have to be passed on under the full gaze of officialdom. Winding up an estate in Spain can be quite involved enough without the added complication of having a foreign will covering Spanish assets, or no will at all.

If an expatriate dies intestate, settling their affairs can be a long drawn-out business and a will made anywhere outside Spain will probably not be much help. A foreign will must, of course, be proved by probate being obtained in the country where it was drawn up and, if Spanish assets are covered, it then has to be translated into Spanish and a decision taken as to whether Spanish or some other legislation applies. And, of course, the question of where the deceased was legally resident affects everything.

Spanish inheritance and capital gains taxes on property can be avoided if the property is owned by a company rather than an individual. This needs to be a Spanish company which, in its turn, is owned by a foreign company. It is not the sort of thing anyone is going to find easy and will obviously involve professional assistance. Some accountants recommend this course, but others have examined the costs and declared that it does not begin to produce any real benefit until the property concerned is in the million-pound range. The reason is that the corporate structure has to be set up and maintained. And while it is a nice thought that simply handing over the company to someone else means that the property does not actually change hands – thereby avoiding any payments and problems – the costs involved may outweigh the taxes that would have been due in the first place.

In the Eighties, there was a trend towards buying Spanish properties through companies set up in offshore centres – Gibraltar was favourite – so that nobody need ever pay the tax levied on transferring property ownership or capital gains tax again. As explained, the ownership of the company was altered but the property still belonged to the company. This popular idea was interrupted by the simple expedient of the Spanish government levying an annual tax of 3 per cent on all property owned by foreign companies, which virtually meant they were collecting the cash every year instead of just when the property was sold.

Transfer tax

The transfer tax when a house changes hands is like the British stamp duty except there is no threshold and it must be paid on the declared value. It is normally 7 per cent of the *escritura de compraventa* (commonly referred to simply as '*escritura*'). This is the value of the property as stated on the title deeds, and it may be quite different from the amount that is actually being paid for it. There may also be a half per cent value added tax (*IVA*) and stamp duty if it is being bought from a developer. These taxes are payable by the buyer. Another tax is levied on the increase in value since the vendor purchased the property … again on any rise in the nominal *escritura* value. This is down to the seller. This *Plusvalía*, as it is called, is dealt with in more detail in Chapter 7.

The transfer tax can cause problems in one unfortunate and sometimes unforeseen fashion. This is when a husband or wife dies and the villa or apartment has been jointly owned, as is often the case with English couples. Technically, they have each owned half the property and – whereas in England the remaining spouse just takes possession of it all – now half of it has to come into the ownership of the survivor named in the deeds and this must be registered. And, of course, a tax of 7 per cent of the value of the property trans-ferred has to be paid … that is, on half of the value of the house. This can come as a nasty shock on top of funeral expenses at a time when pension income is likely to be reduced into the bargain.

Four categories

Under Spanish inheritance law there are four separate categories of inheritors, and any bequest is taxed on a sliding scale according to their relationship to the deceased.

Inheritance tax is levied on anyone benefitting from the will and must be paid inside six months or penalties will be incurred. Settling an estate is complex, for there are 16 levels of tax – starting at 7.65 per cent on the equivalent of around £5,000 and rising to 34 per cent on amounts above about £500,000. Allowances start from about £30,000 for infants reducing with age to £10,000 for descendants up to the age of 21, after which birthday that threshold applies. Those are the first two groups, the descendants or adopted chil-dren under 21 and over 21.

The two other categories are other immediate relatives (brothers, sisters, nephews, nieces, uncles and aunts) whose allowance against tax is the equivalent of about £5,000, and a final category covering anyone not related to the deceased. Beneficiaries in this final category have no allowance at all.

Whereas in Britain a person can leave anything to anyone they like, Spanish law stipulates the proportions which *have* to be left to family members before the remainder can be disposed of as the owner wishes. At least one-third of a person's estate must be left to any surviving children in equal parts. A further third must go to any child or grandchild, but at the testator's choice, but any sur-viving spouse retains a lifetime's interest in that third. The remaining third is the only part that can be dealt with entirely at the donor's discretion.

This means that a husband and wife who have children will see those offspring receive a third of their estate when either of them dies and, while they may or may not be bequeathed a third of whatever their spouse leaves, they are only guaranteed to receive *an interest* in the third which must be passed on at their own death to a child or grandchild. It is clear then that offspring have a far larger say than in the UK as to what happens to a surviving parent or grandparent.

If the value of any real estate is under-declared by the parties, the tax authorities will consider that the difference between their declared value and the one they affix constitutes a gift, and tax both the seller and the buyer on that amount.

All inheritance tax is the liability of the recipient and cannot be taken from the estate of the deceased. This means that the tax must be paid before any bequest is actually received and, as the inheritor does not own the property yet, it cannot be used as security against a loan or sold to meet the bill.

Of course, this means that in the case of a joint account in a bank, half the money in it becomes part of the estate of the deceased. In cases where – as is quite normal in Spanish society – the husband holds the account in his sole name, none of the money can be used by the widow to pay any taxes, or even to live on, as the money in the account is subject to probate.

Capital gains

Capital gains tax is levied in Spain on the increase in value of any property when it changes hands and is payable whether the owner is a Spanish resident or not. Capital gains tax also applies to other items such as stocks and shares, a business or antiques. Losses, like the fees payable on a sale, are eligible to be offset against any capital gain.

One item definitely on the credit side is that any resident over the age of 65 is exempt from capital gains tax on their home. If you are not a pensioner, capital gains tax will not apply if you re-invest at least as much as any sale realises in another Spanish property within three years. Any capital gains tax you are due to pay will be treated as income during the year in which the gain was made if you are a Spanish resident. If any property has been held for less than two years, any gain will be added to other income and taxed accordingly. For non-residents, the rate of tax on this increase is 35 per cent.

One escape clause here is that if the property was bought before 1987, capital gains tax does not apply. Anything bought since then is subject to capital gains tax affected by factors such as whether it is your main residence and whether or not you are a resident.

As has been stated earlier, taxes affecting inheritance and the transfer of property can soon become very complicated in Spain and are areas where it can pay handsomely to seek professional help in the first instance to avoid a lot of worry later on.

Making plans

As with anything else in life, planning is necessary before you make that final decision to 'up sticks' and move the centre of your universe a thousand miles or so to the south. Just how much detail is put into the planning depends on your temperament. Some get involved with minute precautions and plot for every eventuality to the extent that they really need a secretary to handle the ramifications. Others are like the man who put a few belongings into an estate car along with his wife, two children and the dog, crossed the Channel, drove through France and across Spain until he reached the Mediterranean and then tossed up whether to go right or left on the coastal highway. Yes, that actually did happen!

You will want to take family treasures with you and probably special items of furniture but, unless you are really attached to a bedroom suite or a table and chairs, it will almost certainly not be worthwhile taking everything. Spanish houses are normally sold complete with the furniture, only things like pictures, household linen and pots and pans being removed. It's a good idea to have everything in writing before you buy so you know just what is included in the sale but, unless you are moving into a newly-built property, you won't need all the contents of your home as you would if moving inside Britain. Even with a new home, the cost of transporting your personal furnishings would go a long way towards buying new items in Spain. A part load to carry what you really want, rather than having everything packed up and carted, can save a lot of money.

Removal firms

Several firms specialise in overseas moves and it pays to seek a quote from one or two before agreeing a contract. It used to be a complicated procedure with legal declarations of what was being carried and lists for bond clearance at the border. The European Union changed all that.

The Consulate

In fact, there is scarcely a thing you *must* do before leaving Britain. It used to be necessary to register at one of the Spanish consulates, but with the coming of the European Union that is no longer a legal formality. There is no legal requirement to register at the local British Consulate in Spain either. But it is still a good idea and any information stored there is never passed on without written permission, so you are not giving away your whereabouts to anyone you do not want to have that knowledge.

The thought that such information is only useful in times of civil unrest – and with such an event unrealistic in the modern Spain – may make registering seem a waste of time. However, no one knows about those events termed 'natural disasters' when details about you could be vital. And the Mediterranean coast of Spain is an earthquake zone. Small readings are often registered by seismology departments at a university or two while quakes violent enough to be felt by the general public are not that rare. That is not the main reason for being on a consulate card, though.

The big advantage comes when something unforeseen does happen and either the person in Spain or their next of kin in the UK needs to be contacted. Having such information to hand has avoided the expensive business of having to store a body while exhaustive inquiries are made, for instance. Quite a few people do die while in Spain without any known next of kin and some with no details registered either.

It is important, too, to keep the details listed with your local consulate current. If you move, tell them. If you go back to the UK, tell them. You can do it by phone if necessary. In terms of the practical advantages, it really is in the interests of all law-abiding citizens to do this.

Now it is more important than it was five or ten years ago to keep details up-to-date with your local consulate because in the last three years there has been no space on the passport application form for next of kin. This has made tracing people more difficult and it will become increasingly difficult as new passports replace existing ones.

Language

'Do we need to speak the language?' This is a question everyone contemplating the move asks. The answer is, of course, that for many the language barrier represents a problem and is definitely on the contrary side. How well or whether you want to learn Spanish depends on the degree to which you want to integrate into Spanish life. Think of those who have moved into Britain who don't speak English and what they miss out on. Even a little ability in the native tongue is a blessing anywhere and though in the major areas of expatriate settlement in Spain many enjoy life with no more than a modicum of Spanish, a rule of thumb is that the more you understand of what is being said around you, the easier things become.

Most people find that the older they are before they start to learn another language, the harder it is. But don't make that an excuse because a few words of Spanish and a smile can go a long way towards securing a welcome. It is a two-way thing, though, and you will come across many instances where the Spanish who want the custom of British clients have no more firm a grasp of your language than you have of theirs.

Many lovely examples of the misuse of languages by those not native to them exist and anyone can end up with a foot in their mouth in all innocence. Like the Spanish lady who opened a kindergarten and wanted English-speaking children too. She put a notice in her window which read: 'We execute your children'. This was not exactly what she meant – we hope!

Menus are a favourite source of much well-meaning muddle and with French, German, Italian and even Russian alongside the English and Spanish, scope for clangers is almost unlimited. One fine sample concerned a dish of monkfish, which in Spanish is *rape* and, though pronounced rah-pay, looks like something else. One method of preparation is known as *marinero* and when this was literally translated and the fish was not, it ended up as 'rape sailor-style.'

Shop signs can cause amusement too. Like the one at the vegetable counter when the scales went wrong which told customers, 'Your vegetables wait at the check-out.' Then there was the Englishman wanting creosote to protect a fence who worked out that he needed wood preserver and translated it as *preservativo de madera*. This brought the ironmonger's to a standstill, and he is always remembered as the man who asked for a wooden condom!

In matters of health, there is the famous (or infamous) *constipado* – which does not mean what you might expect, but refers to a cold. Nor are private dinner parties exempt. An English lady told her Spanish neighbour at table that she had bought her son a pedometer and wondered why everyone laughed at his question as to whether it was to measure the sound or the volume. Then they pointed out that in Spanish the word *pedo* means 'I break wind'!

It's all too easy to get it wrong, but the best advice is to go ahead and take a chance anyway. Incidentally, it says something about the Spanish character that there is no straight translation for the word 'wrong' in the sense that you can tell someone when they are. It probably saves an awful lot of violence. The nearest you can get is '*No tiene razón*' (literally 'you don't have reason') but do be careful when and where you use it.

There is a further complication. While most foreigners think of Spanish (Castilian) as the language of the country, there are actually *four* legal languages in Spain: Castilian, Basque, Catalan and Galician. However, the last three of these are spoken in their regions only, so unless you are moving to one of these areas you will be as likely to encounter these languages as you would be to meet a native Welsh speaker in Surrey. All things considered, you are unlikely to meet anyone who will not at least understand the Spanish you find on language tapes.

The pace of life

One benefit about life in Spain, which is quoted by many, is that the pace of life is slower than in the UK, though when you are caught up in the maelstrom of traffic in Madrid, Barcelona or a dozen other major cities it is not easy to accept. The fact is that the Spanish give priority to the important things that make life more enjoyable. Things like eating and chatting with friends, forgetting all about work once knocking-off time comes and taking every excuse for a *fiesta*. Perhaps it is this trait which affects time for, although it is supposed to be a constant, it does seem to pass differently south of the Pyrenees … it goes more quickly!

It is a good idea to remember that the reason some people find it hard to settle in Spain is the fact that they arrive with rose-tinted spectacles instead of sunglasses. It has to be remembered that nowhere this side of the Pearly Gates is all 'pros' and that there are always at least a few 'cons'. Accepting that you will not leave all your problems in the UK and that you will be swapping one lot for another will speed the transfer to a new life in the sun. For most folk, though, any fresh obstacles on the way to a healthy retirement are infinitely preferable to the old ones.

One definite plus is that you will never have to bother with a television licence again – or worry about somebody in a detector van trying to land you with a £2,000 fine. In Spain you just buy your set and watch it. And what there is to watch will be looked at in more detail in Chapter 10.

2 Where do they come from?

The multi-national mix

Moving into any of the tourist areas of Spain, which is where most expatriates retire to, is to join a truly international community. You will probably make sure you have plenty of fellow countrymen around and, of course, you will encounter lots of Spaniards who have lived in the area for generations. But you will find yourself part of the melting pot of nations which Spain's Mediterranean coast has become.

How far you want to integrate is up to you. Some English spend many years in the country without gaining much of a grip on the local customs or language and certainly never attempt a conversation with a Spaniard – unless it is with one of the many who have taken the time to learn English. And they still enjoy life and get a lot out of it.

The truth is that we British are generally lazy when it comes to learning another tongue. The widely accepted view that learning a language becomes more difficult with age may well be just a myth, but it is a view that many find a convenient excuse for speaking only English. To some extent it is the foreigners who have made English-speakers like this for, whenever the British try to use whatever other language they have studied almost anywhere in the world, the locals will want to practise their English on them. That's much easier; they are usually better at it in any case than the British are when spluttering away with theirs. So, English it is! However, if you wish to experience your adopted country as fully as possible, you should make every effort to learn the language as this will enhance your understanding of its people and its culture.

It is a fact that many of the Germans, French, Belgians and Scandinavians you will be living among, speak our language – and all the Dutch do. You will find yourself rubbing shoulders with them all and our mother tongue is the unifying link.

Take a random example. The villa in question is on an urbanisation, which is one of those communities where the roads, lighting and a swimming pool are shared by those who own property on the development. Across the road, in two houses which used to belong to two Finnish couples, are a growing Spanish family who have virtually combined the properties and extended the total living space to their liking. And the building work has been done by a Ukrainian. Next door is a Spanish man who works in a hotel where he met his Finnish wife who is in the travel industry.

On the other side is the holiday home of a Swede – which he bought from a South African couple – and he is married to a Rumanian. Beyond them is a house inhabited by a German couple and their son, while English, Irish and Scottish families are further along the street. A retired Spanish couple, a lady from Ecuador, another from Switzerland, an Italian married to a Spaniard, a Gibraltarian who has a getaway from the Rock, a couple of Welsh pensioners, and a retired American serviceman are among the predominantly English people who have moved in permanently or have second homes there.

Residencias

Many of the expatriates, but not all, will have gone through the process of getting their *tarjeta de residente comunitario*, known by all and sundry as a *residencia*, that is their identity card. All Spaniards have an ID card and are required to show it to prove who they are in many instances. For example, if they are not known in a shop or supermarket where they intend to pay with a credit card, it is their national identity card that will be produced to back up the transaction. The British have no such thing and when identification is required are expected to prove who they are by showing their passport, or their *residencia* if they have one.

However, when you become a resident in Spain, you are required to apply for this *residencia* if you are not exempt (see below). Once Spain had joined the European Union it was hoped this would no longer be the case. After all, it was argued, citizens of other countries covered by the Treaty of Rome, like the British, have the right to live in Spain or anywhere else now. That has not proved to be the case, however, and the expatriate pensioner still needs this card to be legally resident in Spain. As its name implies, it regularises the position of someone residing in Spain. It means they can have a Spanish driving licence; can pay tax in Spain instead of elsewhere (which may or may not be an advantage); become exempt from certain taxes on foreigners; can receive a number which facilitates opening a bank account; and, at least in theory, can expect to be treated as a Spanish citizen.

The card, which has to be renewed every five years, is obtained at the station of the National Police which is designated for the area where the new arrival intends to live and is taking up domicile. They must present an array of documents and photographs. This tends to change a little and it is best to obtain a list of the latest up-to-date requirements. Normally they will consist of:

1   Your passport and a photocopy
2   Proof of medical insurance
3   Proof of pension
4   Proof of means of support
5   Four photos
6   A fee of €6.19 (see below)

The passport and one photocopy are self-explanatory. In fact, it is a good idea to have a photocopy of every piece of paper, just in case. There is a belief that some *residencia* offices enjoy insisting that something is missing, thus keeping the applicant running around. A subterfuge which may triumph over this gambit is to deliberately hold back something requested, like one of the photos or the passport photocopy. When the clerical official slaps down their ace that you are an item short, the person on the other side of the counter can trump it by discovering that they have it all the time. With any luck, that will settle the matter.

The form E121 for State Retirement pensioners, their spouses and dependent children, and for anyone receiving a UK Incapacity Benefit, is all the medical cover necessary. The E111, for those below pensionable age, may not be regarded as sufficient in some cases so private cover will be necessary. (See the section on health forms in Chapter 12.)

A way of proving you are in receipt of a UK state pension is to have it paid into your Spanish bank account, and then take along a letter stamped by the bank to show you are receiving one. If your pension is paid in this way, the bank should not charge commission, though some do. If it is paid into a bank outside Spain and money brought in to pay your bills as needed, a letter from your Spanish bank stating how much you have in your account will suffice.

The number of photographs – passport size and type – has varied but it has tended to settle at four. There is considerable speculation as to what they are all for. It is obvious one is wanted for the *residencia* itself and a second is attached to the application form which is probably filed away somewhere for the future, but why four have to be provided is generally supposed to be because that is the number turned out by the passport photo booths where most of them are taken and it would be a pity to have an odd one or two left over. Anyway, four it is.

The fee of €6.19 was correct at the beginning of 2003, but it is different for people from countries outside the EU and could be subject to alteration. It is not handed over at the police station where the application is dealt with but can be paid in at any bank – the one nearest the police station is likely to be most familiar with the procedure. The bank will retain one copy of the form you have filled in, in triplicate, and this is stamped to show you have paid this peculiar amount.

What must be handed over?

If a couple are applying for *residencias* and one of them does not have their own separate pension, a marriage certificate (again with its accompanying photocopy) must be produced.

It sounds onerous but, once embarked upon, the process is not as daunting as it appears. Indeed, the whole endeavour can be avoided by hiring a *gestor* – a specialist in paperwork – to do it all for you. But the charge is off-putting – especially if a couple is involved – and the rigmarole does provide an introduction for many into the world of Spanish bureaucracy. A month or so afterwards (though in some parts of Spain this can be as long as nine months) you will have to appear in person in any case, for the recipient must put their fingerprint on it – and nobody else can do that.

Once you have one, it is necessary to go through the whole business again when its expiry date approaches, starting about a month before the current identity card expires. Technically there is a fine of £3,000 for failing to do so. There is also a move afoot to try and make British pensioners exempt from needing a *residencia* at all as they have every right to live in Spain with health cover available, and so on. Various bodies representing foreign residents are examining the possibilities but, for the time being, that form-filling awaits.

The exempt

A new law passed in the Spanish Parliament on 14 February 2003 exempts some foreigners from all this hassle. It should be in operation by the time this book comes out, but it remains to be seen just how it will be applied. The new royal decree removes the requirement to have a *residencia* from those who have paid into the state's social security system.

Any European Union citizen – as well as those from Norway, Liechtenstein, Switzerland and Iceland – who is living in Spain and is employed or self-employed, is a student, a pensioner or a retired person who has paid the Spanish social security taxes, is exempt. Those no longer obliged to have a *residencia* also include the direct family members of those listed. Those from the European Community who have never, at any time, worked in Spain will still need to obtain the residency card.

Those who meet the conditions set out in the new law and currently live in Spain should not need to renew their card when it runs out. Anyone who returns to Spain in the future and meets the requirements will not need to apply for a residency card at all.

The royal decree had its origin in an agreement reached in July 2000, between Spain, France, Germany and Italy, under which those in possession of an identification card or passport issued in their own country would be able to reside in Spain and – providing they met the above mentioned conditions – need not apply for any further document. In the case of Britons, who were included in the Spanish law newly enacted, a passport would be the only thing necessary to perform monetary transactions or apply for a driving licence.

How many foreigners are there?

So, how many non-Spanish residents are there living in Spain? The answer is that nobody knows. A commonly accepted figure that is bandied about by real estate companies and holiday firms is that there are 700,000 British expatriates living in Spain. However, this is based on how many homes are owned by holders of British passports and includes some time-share, fortnight-at-a-time, investments along with other accommodation used for holiday visits and not full-time living. This is then multiplied by how many people are involved per property which is, again, another figure difficult to quantify accurately. The result is that this near three-quarters of a million figure – which may be as near as anyone can get – is approximate at best. And, of course, that is only the Brits!

As far as we – the British – are concerned, the best estimate from our own representatives in the country is that only something like 10 per cent of the UK citizens living full-time in Spain have actually taken out residency or registered at the local town hall. Taking one of the most popular parts of the land for Britons as an example there are, in round figures, 30,000 living legally registered on the Costa del Sol. It is generally accepted, however, that ten times that number are actually there permanently at any one time without any registration whatsoever.

A similar situation is accepted as existing for all the other nationalities and no one is sure how many Scandinavians, Germans, Belgians and Dutch – who make up the bulk of expatriates along with the Brits – are there, let alone the non-European Union folk from Eastern Europe, Africa, America (North, South and Central) and the Middle and Far East.

Figures provided by one of the resorts which benefits from this foreign influx could well be taken as a mark of where the proportion of foreigners come from. These are residents who are *empadronados*, that is, who have registered at the town hall, and details of just what that means and how you should be listed are given in Chapter 8 on Town Halls and Taxes. Among the Europeans there are 1,236 from the United Kingdom and Northern Ireland, 29 from the Irish Republic, 1 from Andorra, 20 Austrians, 103 Belgians, 2 from Bulgaria, 297 Danes, 153 from Finland, 82 French, 1 Greek, 6 from Iceland, 57 Italians, 1 from Luxemburg, 141 Dutch, 4 from Poland, 20 from Portugal, 21 Germans, 2 Romanians, 143 Swedes, 22 Swiss, 4 from the former USSR, and 6 from what used to be Yugoslavia.

A total of 176 people from 10 African countries are also listed, with the vast majority being the 158 from Morocco. The USA has 65 on the list, Canada 14 and Mexico just 3. Ten South American countries are also represented with the bulk of the 191 made up of 138 from Argentina. Four Australians have registered while Asia has 157 on the list including 31 from the Philippines, 20 from China and 59 from Iran. Multiply that number by 10, reckon the local consulates, and you are getting nearer the actual numbers in each case.

What are they worth?

All these immigrants form a vital resource as far as the financial running of the area is concerned. In a bid to get a grip on things a decade ago, a committee on tourism in one of the coastal regional governments came up with the figure that each 'residential tourist' was worth 20 times as much to the local economy as a holiday-maker. That figure was immediately questioned and is demonstrably way too low. What is it worth when someone decides to buy a house or an apartment to live in or takes out a rental contract in Spain? Someone running a car, buying all their groceries, paying their insurance, taxes and rates, electricity and telephone bills ... the net worth is clearly many times greater than the contribution of someone staying in a hotel for a couple of weeks.

The problem is that all the tourist information is based on hotel accommodation as that is the only figure that is something concrete on which to base decisions. And those decisions are taken by regional tourist councils made up – that's right – almost entirely of representatives of the hotel industry!

Things are not made easier by the fluid nature of the population either for there is a constant change-over of those moving in and those returning home or heading for pastures new. Neither is officialdom helpful, for to be a resident in Spain you must spend at least 183 days in any calendar year in the country, while you are considered resident in the UK if you are there for more than 91 days in a year. Lots of people, who spend part of the year in a home in each of the countries, could qualify as being resident in both places.

Thanks to a reciprocal agreement, tax need only be paid in one or other country but, due to the freedom of cross-border movement that arrived with the European Union, it is virtually impossible to know just where all the citizens of the various countries in Europe actually are.

This residential movement, rather than just a holiday visit, blossomed alongside the growth of travel due to affordable airfares. Through the 1950s, it gathered pace and swelled during the next three decades as more and more people found they did not have to put up with northern winters and began to settle full-time in the sun. The recession which bit into the European economy in the early 1990s slowed this flood to a trickle. One real estate agent who had established a reputation for fair dealing and had done well during those boom years, survived the lean spell in spite of not selling a single property for six months during that period.

The delivery vans which had brought tons of furniture from Britain for expatriates heading south and had generally returned empty, found things had gone into reverse. Folk who could no longer afford two homes or who had to return to Britain as their money would not stretch the way it had, were now filling the vehicles on the north-ward journeys and the lorries were unladen on the way south.

Indeed, at the height of this exodus one wag erected a sign on the main road heading to Madrid from the south which read 'Will the last person to leave the Costa del Sol please switch the light off'.

Tall indicators

This barometer, that reflects the health of the south of Spain, has reversed again though and making the momentous move is once more finding favour with thousands. Another indicator of how things are progressing is to count the number of tower cranes employed on building projects along the *costas*. Ten years ago, there were few on site as the Spanish banks had put a block on providing loans for speculative development. Now this expensive equipment, which swings masses of material on to lofty scaffolding, is everywhere. From one market place recently an estate agent, who had suggested to some folk he was showing round that they try this as a gauge, found them double checking when they tallied more than 20 on the skyline from that single spot.

Most of the provision of homes for people wishing to live by the Mediterranean is, of course, along the coastal strip which, for much of its length all the way from France to Portugal, is hemmed in and kept narrow by mountains. Buyers are more and more coming from within Spain itself, too, as the relatively recent mercenary trend allows those from the north of the country to take out mortgages for holiday accommodation and eventual retirement property, while those newly affluent in the southern cities are moving out of the tower blocks into townhouses and villas on new developments. You could say that Spain itself has discovered the *costas* in recent years.

There is, too, a movement inland with villages within easy commuting distance of coastal conurbations and convenient for holiday amenities being opened up to a whole new set of citizens. Those who take up this rural life are more likely to be expatriates who have lived on the coast for some time and feel secure enough in totally Spanish surroundings to join in the local scheme of things, something which is not easy to do when arriving in the country with no previous first-hand experience of its customs or how Spanish is spoken in the neighbourhood. Some do find the space and peace of the mountains to their liking, however, while others revel in being '*El Ingles*' among their fellow citizens in a true Spanish environment.

3 The differences

Getting a new name

Anyone who has spent even the shortest of holidays in Spain is bound to have noticed many facets of life which are just not the same as they have been used to. And when you get to live in the land, you will find these differences cut much deeper than merely driving on the 'wrong' side of the road and arguing about bullfighting.

Ken Chambers, for example, had been waiting at the clinic for hours. Now, he had reached the point where he had made up his mind to put his limited Spanish to use and find out why he was being ignored. All the others whose appointments were for 10 o'clock had been dealt with. So had those with 10.30 and 11 on their papers.

As he approached the desk, he saw the only name not crossed out on the receptionist's clipboard was his. There it was 'Kenneth Richard Chambers' as large as life. So why hadn't she called him?

She had, she told him; but apparently he hadn't been there. 'I call *Señor* Reecher,' she said, 'but nobody answer'.

Ken was about to learn that, in Spain, most people have two surnames and one Christian name. The receptionist had called his name as she had all the others on her list, the middle name being the one they all answered to – except Ken. He had not recognised her pronunciation of his middle name while looking out for 'Chambers'.

Forms in Spain leave space for one Christian name – the *nombre*. But there are two spaces for surnames – the first and second *apellidos*. The first is that of the person's father and the second that of the mother, both family surnames being used. Northern Europeans just have to get used to their second Christian name being used as their surname whenever their full names are written down … unless they fill in the form wrongly by accident or on purpose. For those with no middle name, the problem does not arise.

Confusion in British minds can also result from the fact that Spanish women do not give up their surname when they marry. So a husband and wife usually have different surnames, even when they are not just 'partners'.

Christian names can be very different, too, with the likelihood that if you were to stand in a busy square in any town and shout 'María!' every woman within earshot would look round. The Virgin's name is very commonly used and because of this, many have combinations they answer to, like *María José*, which is Mary-Jo, while her brother could just as easily be *José María*. There are colourful combinations as well, like *María del Mar* (literally Mary of the Sea), *María del Castillo* (Mary of the Castle) or *María de las Nieves* (Mary of the Snows, whose picturesque name recalls our Snow White).

Many Spanish men bear the name *Jesús* and because its pronunciation (He-zoose) makes it sound similar, it can be called instead of our 'Bless you!' when somebody sneezes. In some regions, if a sneezing fit goes on though you can continue the blessing in Spanish by adding, successively, *María! José*! And if any more are required, *Todos los Santos*! (All the Saints!)

Wedding rings

Another significant difference is that the ladies in many parts of Spain wear their wedding rings on the third finger of their *right* hand. I am informed that in Murcia, Valencia, Gerona and the Balearics this is not the case, while the women of Madrid wear their rings on the right hand unless widowed when they change them to the left. This can mean that, in early days living among Spaniards, it can be easy to overlook the fact that someone is married and call them *señorita* instead of *señora*. Sometimes the same, plain, gold band is worn on the left hand when a girl is engaged and then switched to the right hand at the wedding. However, the idea of having a separate engagement ring is popular too, and that is worn on the right hand. It can be confusing and, of course, it is easy for a Spaniard to think a foreign lady is single if she has the ring on the wrong hand – which to them may be her left one.

Days of the week

Other simpler things can also lead to misunderstandings. For example, Monday (*lunes*) is the first day of the week on Spanish calendars, not Sunday (*domingo*). And it is not Friday (*viernes*) the thirteenth that is unlucky in Iberia. The day you have to beware of in Spain is when the thirteenth falls on a Tuesday (*martes*). Incidentally, the other days of the week are Wednesday (*miércoles*), Thursday (*jueves*) and Saturday (*sábado*). And you will notice that they are all spelt without a capital letter.

The fact that a blue joke is a *green* one to a Spaniard may account for the difficulty the Green Party has in being taken as seriously in elections as it would like.

Rubbish collection

As for household refuse, the bin men do not call once a week and empty your own personal dustbin. You must take it to one of the special skips which are strategically placed alongside roads and outside premises. This is not as onerous as it at first appears as it is easy to take a plastic bagful and pop it in whenever you go out, for the local council staff make a collection every day. It is actually more hygienic than having your waste stored outside your door when you think about it, especially in the summer heat. But beware! In some areas there are rules about not putting anything into the *basuras* as they are called until, say, nine o'clock in the evening. Some councils also set aside special days which are the only ones when they will cart away furniture or garden rubbish left by the bins.

Many authorities are also doing their bit for the environment nowadays by providing bottle banks and special containers for, for example, paper and cardboard, or batteries. Use them, for you may be the only foreigner your Spanish neighbours see dumping their rubbish and then they will think all Brits are as considerate as you are.

When you are buying a house or looking for a flat to rent, it is a good idea to note where these bins are, not necessarily because you don't want to carry rubbish any further than you have to, but because they can be emptied at some funny hours and it is not the quietest of operations.

Noise and conversations

This leads us on to the subject of noise. Everyone notices that the Spanish make more of it than we do. It is partly to do with living a more open-air existence and, of course, with doors and windows open, more sound is bound to be heard outside. And children, who must keep out of the heat in the middle of hot summer days, have to play some time – which is why you may hear games and skipping going on at a time when all good English children are tucked up in bed. But there is more to it than that.

Take the average British pub, for example. Even when there are lots of people in there, most of the conversations are carried on round tables in a relatively normal tone and there are dirty looks when anybody gets a bit too boisterous. In Spanish bars it is totally different. Everybody talks at once and, to make themselves heard, they all have to shout louder than the next person. So the volume rises.

The Spanish conversation is a wonderful thing, for with all participants interrupting one another and making points at the same time, they still seem to follow what is being said all around them. This is an art most expatriates find beyond them.

This ability to concentrate on a conversation to the exclusion of all else does have its drawbacks, however. Not wishing to become embroiled in a hackneyed debate about women drivers, it is perhaps best just to pass on a comment from a Spanish insurance agent. He pointed out that from investigating many claims, it was apparent that whenever there are two Spanish women in a car together you have a potential calamity on your hands because the one who is driving will be much more interested in the chat with her companion than anything that could possibly be going on outside the car. The point might also be made that Spanish men can enjoy a good chat too!

Then there are the motor bikes … but they will be dealt with in a later chapter on common complaints.

Driving on the 'wrong' side

On roads in general, driving on the right rather than on the left leads to several fatalities and serious injuries every year, not so much because of drivers being on the wrong side but because pedestrians are looking the wrong way when they step off the pavement in front of a moving vehicle. That 'Right, left, right' we have been doing since we were old enough to be let out on our own, must become 'Left, right, left'.

Drivers normally soon overcome the change – once they stop grabbing the window winder with their left hand instead of the gear shift with their right. But lots of passengers carry on getting into the left hand door for years and wondering what the steering wheel is doing in their lap.

'Plugging in'

Holiday visitors to Spain will know that electric sockets are not the same as they are in the UK and that you have to take an adaptor with you if you want to use an electric shaver or a hair drier. When you move to live in the country, however, any electric appliances you take with you will need a new plug of the round pinned Continental type rather than the rectangular ones they had before.

You can, of course, fit an adaptor on every plug and carry on, but sooner or later there will come a day when an extension lead or some gadget or other will not connect to something else. Better to become totally switched on to round pins, change over completely and give your British plugs to a friend who will still need them. Spanish plugs are not fused as are those in use in the UK, but that is not a cause for concern because the system to which they connect your television or refrigerator is protected already.

Trip switches are installed anywhere that a mains supply enters premises. In the average home, there will be one that covers the entire circuit with smaller ones in the panel that protect the kitchen, main living area and bedrooms separately. If you get something overheating or there is a short circuit, the switch drops immediately and stops the current. If there is a power cut with a subsequent surge in the power or if an incident – like lightning striking a sub-station – occurs, the main switch will be knocked out to prevent damage to installations. Once power is back on, just push the switch or switches back up and all is normal.

If there is going to be any damage caused to apparatus it is likely to be when the power comes back on with a wallop after there has been an interruption in the supply. This can jolt sensitive equipment and it is a good idea to have a surge protector in the line; certainly it is advisable to have one stabilising the current to a computer.

Some opt for the belt-and-braces approach of having a Spanish plug but with an English socket at the end of a length of cable into which their UK plug is fitted. With a three or five amp fuse in that, a television, for instance, is doubly protected.

The Spanish system causes no problems in modern buildings but in some older properties it is possible that the trip switch fitted when electricity was installed several years ago may not be strong enough to cope with the demands made by all the electrical appliances in the modern home. For example, another room or two added on since the original electrical system was put in will have increased the current called for. If only lighting or a radio is used, the extra juice needed will not amount to much. But a reason for irritation in several instances is that microwave ovens had not been thought of then. It may be that if a fridge, a television and a computer are being used at the same time as a kettle and an oven in the kitchen, and then a microwave is turned on, the major input into it may take the total required to a level which will make the trip switch do its job of protecting things by turning everything off. If this happens a time or two, the answer is a new control box on the power coming into the home, probably 40 amps instead of 30 or even 20.

Holy days

The Spanish attitude to religion is one area where the cultural gap is most easily identified. Even Roman Catholics from northern lands find some forms of worship within Iberian Catholicism outside their experience, while an Anglo-Saxon Protestant may well consider some of the local practices tantamount to idolatry. The Reformation, which removed the worship of saints from the northern churches' rituals, had no effect here and local saints are honoured throughout the land.

All towns and villages have their patron saint and their holiday is duly recognised by a fair – the *feria*. The effigy of this saint or the local Virgin is kept for the rest of the year in the local church or a hermitage nearby but paraded for this celebration. It may be an ornate affair or barely noticed in the jollification caused by the fairground rides which descend on the municipality for the duration. In many communities the saint is also paraded through the streets during *Semana Santa*, the Holy Week of Easter.

In Andalucía especially, the solemn ritual of carrying representations of saints, the Virgin or scenes of Christ's crucifixion, brings huge crowds to the streets of major cities such as Málaga, Sevilla, Córdoba and Granada with wide television coverage. Some of these are borne by members of brotherhoods with a hundred or more getting sore shoulders from the effort, for some of these ornate creations weigh tons.

Corpus Cristi is another occasion honoured in June by many places and an ancient festival honouring Carmen, who protects fishermen, is a summer *fiesta* in coastal towns. As well as each town, every individual has their own saint's day, too. Though the custom is perhaps not as widely followed in these secular times as it used to be, the child's name gives it a day of its own as well as its birthday. You may still find a clerk named *Julián* missing from the town hall on 9th January, for instance, for that is the day of his patron.

(Incidentally, if you have the name Cyril like me, which is *Cirilo* in Spain, you can claim three days – 27th June for *Cirilo de Alejandría*, 18th March for *Cirilo de Jerusalén* and 14th February which *Cirilo* shares with that late-coming interloper Valentine.)

Just in case you don't know when your saint's day falls, there is the encompassing All Saints' Day on 1st November, which is a national Bank Holiday. Whereas the Americans go trick-or-treating on Halloween, the Spanish make the most of the day itself. Families make their way to the local cemetery to commune with deceased parents or grandparents and even have picnics among the freshly-cleaned and flower-bright niches where their loved ones' remains have been laid to rest.

It has been said by some observers that the Spanish have a love affair with death. Be that as it may, there is something heartwarming about this unwillingness to let go the fond memories of recent ancestors.

Something else you will come across when you live in Spain is the *puente*. Literally meaning a bridge, the word is used in connection with bank holidays and saints' days whenever they fall on a Tuesday or a Thursday. Then, for some, the intervening Monday or Friday becomes a *puente*. It does not affect shops and factories too much, but many building firms deem it not worth while to start things moving again just for one day and turn the day-long break into a four-day weekend.

Christmas is a one-day affair in many parts of Spain (though in the Balearics, Cataluña and some parts of Valencia, the 26th is also a holiday). However, the lack of Boxing Day is more than made up for by Constitution Day on 6 December, the Immaculate Conception on

8 December and Epiphany, the festival of the Three Kings, on 6 January – as well as New Year's Day, of course.

In fact, 6 January, *El Dia de Los Reyes*, is a very important day for Spanish families for that is when children receive their gifts, marking the offerings for the infant Jesus which the Wise Men brought that first Christmas rather than having their presents on Christmas Day itself as is the custom in the UK. Floats bearing the three kings, who throw sweets to the children, tour the streets of many towns during the evening of 5 January.

In some parts of Spain – particularly in Valencia – religious fervour is shown by the re-enactment of ancient battles between Christians and the Moors. Though the way it is portrayed may be different, the message is still that they wish to express their gratitude to the Virgin for the victories of many centuries ago.

And yet religious tolerance is much in evidence with synagogues in every community which has a Jewish population, Protestant churches wherever expatriates want them, mosques anywhere that Arab inhabitants can sustain one, and even Buddhist temples and Hindu pagodas appearing among the holiday hotels.

Food

When a Spanish colleague asked an Englishman, 'What do you eat at home?' the conversation that followed showed clearly that he imagined Brits live entirely on roast beef and Yorkshire pudding with the odd cod and chips to break the monotony. It was pointed out that this was no more true than that he ate nothing but *paella*, sardines and tomatoes.

The truth is that the Spanish now enjoy a wider choice of menu than ever before – just as the rest of the world does. Retailers are not slow to learn that where there are numbers of foreign residents, they appreciate things that are familiar to them which were not available in that area before. And the locals are not averse to trying them to see what they are like and, if they find them to their taste, incorporating this addition into their diet.

Items like tea, custard powder and Marmite used to be unobtainable and brought out by friends or their purchase included in a run down the coast to visit a bank in Gibraltar. But they are now on the shelves of supermarket chains wherever there is a high concentration of British expatriates. In fact, there is little that is not available in any area where the British have settled, from jars bearing familiar labels that contain jam to popular brands of flour. These imported goods are, of course, more expensive for those who insist on remaining with brands they are used to rather than making use of locally produced alternatives.

Much has been said about 'The Mediterranean Diet'. However, the younger generation of Spaniards would seem happy to exist on a diet made up entirely of pizzas, hamburgers, chips and Coke, just as these fast foods have carved a similar niche elsewhere. But the prized and healthy lifestyle of yesteryear can still be enjoyed throughout Spain.

Olive oil

Unlike in Britain, two nutritious ingredients are the base of any culinary activity – olive oil and garlic. Many are the brands of olive oil on offer. Some come from large co-operatives while others are much more expensively presented produce from select groves that promise distinctive flavours. It is much like wines really. One thing they all have in common though is that they are much cheaper than olive oil available in the UK.

Most chefs have their own favourite and claim that it is a factor in their dishes having a distinctive character. Be that as it may, the answer is to try a few until you find one you like. The oil comes in various grades with the extra virgin from the first pressing being the best and dearest, the bulk of the oil – which is by no means second rate but less expensive – being the most commonly used. A cheap, end-of-run squeezing that includes essence from the crushed stones, brings up the rear. The oil comes in sizes from tiny, tempting bottles to gallon plastic containers.

It has been claimed that the olive – with the need to stay in one place to guard and tend the trees – was the prime cause of our civilisation evolving, for it made the nomadic hunter settle down and build houses and fortifications. Its early use was not confined to its flavour or nutritional value either. Until relatively recently, it was also in demand as a source of light. Olive oil lamps lit ancient Rome, for example, with much of the oil coming from their Iberian colonies. This was established when modern scientific methods proved that many thousands of amphora, those storage vessels of the ancients, which had brought oil to Rome and then been discarded, had been made from southern Spanish clay.

Jaen, the most northern of Andalucía's provinces, is still the world's most intensive olive-growing area and it is possible to drive for hours through undulating countryside covered entirely with millions of trees. Many other vast tracts of Spanish land are olive-green thanks to a cloak of the trees and their spread is not in decline either. European Union subsidies for olive growers used to be based on the weight of olives harvested, which left some of the less productive Greek and Italian growers at a disadvantage. So, at the end of the Nineties, the system was changed with production encouraged by the subsidy being paid on the number of trees. This has led to fresh orchards being planted with the official hand-outs giving a return during the years before the trees yield a worthwhile crop. Whoever is counting the billions of trees between Madrid and the Spanish coast won't be redundant for a year or two!

The olives themselves are available with or without stones and stuffed with pepper or anchovy. They form part of many dishes or are eaten as a delicious accompaniment to cheese or a slice of sausage. They are sold loose – which gives you the chance to try before buying – or in tins or jars.

Sunflower oil is always available as well and many British pallets prefer this for its less intrusive taste and the fact that it has a higher flashpoint in the pan which makes it less demanding to use. Incidentally, if you travel around inland Spain during the summer you will see fields and fields of sunflowers, not so called just because of their bright yellow faces. They owe their name to the fact that they always face towards the sun. If you drive through an area with fields on either side of the road, you can find yourself looking at all yellow flowers on one side, and nothing but green as they turn their backs towards you on the other.

Garlic

Anyone who cooks will know all about garlic these days. It is just that if you want your cooking to be Spanish, you will have to use lots more of it. On buses or trains you will normally catch a whiff of it from some of your fellow passengers. They may well have eaten some raw for breakfast, for the traditional start of the day consists of a toasted roll with either crushed or whole garlic cloves on it, a soaking of olive oil and a slice of tomato. This, or a variation of it with *café con leche* (white coffee) was certainly the traditional breakfast in many parts of Spain, but the young of today have different ideas. However, *pa amb oli* – as bread with oil is known in Cataluña and the Balearics – is sufficiently important for Tomás Graves, youngest son of the poet Robert Graves, to have written a book called *Bread and Oil: Majorcan Culture's Last Stand* with an English version published in 2000.

Most Brits can't take this amount of garlic, but a slice of toast and just the right amount of a good, 'nutty' olive oil to soften it without too much running to waste is delicious. Some get their garlic intake by keeping cloves in the bottle with the oil.

Meat products and fish

As for sausages, the choice is huge with all the types available at your local delicatessen counter in England on offer in Spanish supermarkets. In addition, however, you will discover dozens of national brands and local offerings with which you are not familiar. The answer, again, is to try some until you find the one that is your favourite.

Hams are a Spanish speciality with the famous *serrano* at the top of the list. Some of these *pata negra* hams, so named from the black feet of the wild boar from which they come, can cost hundreds of euros. There is an immense choice of Spanish cheeses with which you will not be familiar, too. *Vaca* on the label means it is made from cows' milk, *oveja* designates that sheep's milk has been used, while *cabra* that it is goats' cheese. There are mixtures of them including all three together.

Whatever meat you want, you will find in either specialist butchers' shops or in the supermarket – just as in England. Chickens and pork are good with turkeys on offer all year round and lamb more expensive. British beef is back on the menu after the BSE and foot-and-mouth scares. Prices are comparable with the UK.

Fresh fish, too, is available from fishmongers or in supermarkets where a good selection of frozen fish is also on offer. You will also find fish of varieties you don't know because – as on most of the Continent – housewives are not restricted to a few species as they are in Britain. *Calamares*, which the British don't want to know about as squid, and *pulpo*, which is equally unwelcome as the octopus, are popular all over Spain. Oily sardines and pilchards are cooked over wood fires on beaches for sale in season and it pays to keep an eye open for fresh tuna. Swordfish are a treat, too, when steaks from one of these streamlined creatures can be bought.

Shellfish of all kinds will also be encountered from clams to crabs and lobsters to langoustines, with mussels and several types of shrimp and prawn offered, both cooked and raw.

Drinks – alcoholic and otherwise

And having made reference to wine, it is here worth saying that many fine examples from various parts of Spain are to be found which are seldom seen outside the country. The French do not entertain wines from anywhere else, and neither do the Italians, so – apart from that famous fortified sherry from Jerez which has become an English speciality – little was exported until recently. La Rioja is the region that has done most to promote its vintages, but it is not hard to find equally good wines from other parts of Spain which are just as pleasant an accompaniment to any meal. And don't overlook *cava*. This light and sparkling drink has found many to praise it recently, though it must not be called Champagne as that name is reserved for wines produced in that specific region of France.

While on the subject of alcoholic drinks, it is interesting to note that many Spaniards prefer a glass of beer with their meals and the choice nowadays is all-encompassing with German, English, Mexican and other trans-Atlantic as well as local brews alongside one another on the shelves. Though some fine brandy comes from Jerez, the favourite tipple with which to round off an evening for many south of the Pyrenees is a glass of whisky! And though it's from Scotland, of course, that's much cheaper in Spain, too.

Milk is perhaps more important in the overall scheme of beverages and in Spain you will not find it delivered to the door by a friendly milkman. It is bought from shops like everything else. And you will find an amazing choice of brands with larger supermarkets having more than 50 different bottles and packages. Fresh milk is *fresca*, but most is of the long-life variety with *entera* being full cream, *semi-desnatada* semi-skimmed and *desnatada* skimmed.

And on the subject of deliveries, something else that will not arrive every morning is your newspaper. English papers are available in most areas where Brits abide but even the ones that are printed in Spain these days will cost more than double the UK price.

Fruit and vegetables

The choice of fruit and vegetables is as wide throughout the year as it is in England, though (depending on whereabouts you live) pota-toes can be dearer due to carriage costs while many other things are cheaper. Avocados (*aguacates*), which have become a major crop in recent years, are plentiful and much less expensive while *berenjenas* (aubergines to us and eggplants to Americans) are as plentiful as several sorts of melon. Do try one of the bottle-green *sandías* (watermelons) that can be as big and heavy as a medicine ball, for a slice kept in the refrigerator is like pink ice and as refreshing as anything on a hot day.

Of course, there are peaches, apricots, grapes, apples, oranges and lemons a-plenty, but another fruit to look out for is the delicious *chirimoya*, whose English name of custard-apple describes it to perfection. It is apple-green with a patterned skin that makes it resemble a grenade. When it begins to soften and turn brown, cut it in half and eat the white pulp with a teaspoon, but mind the shiny black seeds of which there can be anything from a couple of dozen to nearly a hundred in the one fruit.

Popular in season, too, is the *nispero*, which is an apricot-looking fruit but with a different flavour. Its English name is the medlar. And pomegranates grow locally, too.

Any consideration of Spanish cuisine must include a discussion about the *tapa*. This Iberian idea makes a cheap snack available in most bars, for behind a glass cover on the counter is an array of trays containing, for example, anchovies in oil, meat balls, eggs in mayonnaise, potato salad and coleslaw. You don't need to know the local names for these dishes. Just point to the ones you want and you will be given a small dish full. If there are a couple of you, you can share half a dozen by helping yourselves with a fork and eating them along with the bread you will be given. A glass of wine or water or a cup of coffee and that's lunch.

If you are more hungry, ask for a '*Ración*' and you will get a bigger, earthenware dish of whatever you point at. These dishes can be shared by all at a table in the same way as a *tapa*. As for paying, when you leave, the dishes will be totted up, and the drinks added to the bill. Easy!

The bullfight

No look at the cultural differences between Spain and the rest of the world could be considered adequate if it did not include reference to that most contentious of issues – the bullfight. *La Corrida*, as it is called locally, has evolved over centuries as a ritual to test the mettle of a man against the ferocity and power of a magnificent animal that has been seen as the symbol of aggression down the ages.

Few rational humans would consent to being enclosed in a confined space with one of them unless he was armed with something at least as lethal as an anti-tank bazooka. That a man will perform traditional manoeuvres with a cape as close to those deadly horns as possible – or risk being derided and booed for his ineptitude – and then dispatch it with a sliver of steel, has to be accepted as courageous. Just as the pageant must be acknowledged to be based on cruelty.

What also has to be accepted is that nobody *has* to go and watch a bullfight.

Just as surely, there are large tracts of Spain that remain unspoiled and preserved simply because they are the territory on which these free-roaming bulls are bred and reared. This is an expensive operation and without the financial return from the eventual presentation of the end product in the arena, these estates would be unsustainable. Beef is provided for the table much more cheaply in other ways.

Some would seek to ban the whole spectacle on grounds of cruelty, while others are addicted to the display of strength and co-ordination. They point to the inherent unpleasantness of slaughterhouses as well and query whether, given the option, many would not choose a pampered life on the plains than be castrated and fattened up for half as long just to avoid 20 minutes of torment at the end … and have the chance to take your tormentor out with you as you go.

It is not a sport, and its depiction in that light has led to much misconception. For sport, there is nothing in Spain to rival football. Indeed, when Barcelona play Real Madrid the entire country is split into opposing camps in much the same way as Glasgow separates into two halves when Rangers and Celtic meet. If Spaniards had to make a decision as to whether soccer or the bulls would have to go, there is little doubt that it would be the end of *La Corrida*. Spain is grateful that it has not had to make the choice.

1992 and all that

Spain's progress into a modern state has been a rapid one. One man virtually decided everything that would be done in the country for 40 years and it is only in the last quarter of a century that the monarchy has established itself, free elections have been held and the economy has changed dramatically. Until the peseta was replaced by the euro in 2002, market traders would still offer goods for sale for '*viente duros*' rather than 100 pesetas. The *duro* was the five-peseta coin just as the 'tanner' was our sixpence and 20 of them made up the required amount. The *duro* – a word meaning 'hard' – was so called because, until well into the second half of the 20th Century, it was what a man got for a hard day's work among the olive or citrus trees. But improvements were coming fast.

The magic year for Spain was to be 1992. Five hundred years after Columbus sailed, a replica of his *Santa María* left Palos on a voyage across the Atlantic; the Olympic Games were held in a completely rebuilt part of Barcelona; the successful EXPO 92 was staged to put Sevilla on the world map; and Spain officially became a full member of the European family. All this led to new roads, improved rail links and a new awareness of Spain's place in the modern world.

It had been anticipated by some that the old rules that meant expatriates had to indulge in a paper chase to become legal were to be wiped away as part of this European integration. But any idea that passports would become a thing of the past and that it would be simple to live anywhere you felt like are still part of that dream of over a decade ago. The paper shufflers are still a long way from redundant.

The vast majority of Spain's income still depends on agriculture as it did in Franco's time with its wine, olive oil, cereal crops, oranges and lemons as important as are its cattle, pig and poultry-rearing and the fishing industry. But tourism plays an ever more important role, as do other service and manufacturing industries. It is almost as if the 200 years since the industrial revolution in Britain have been concentrated into little more than a tenth of that time.

With the new wealth has come a greater freedom. Girls smoke in the street and go into bars, things that would have been severely frowned on in their mothers' young days.

Old men still glance over their shoulder when they can be persuaded to talk about Franco. Diego – who worked in England after his brother and two cousins were killed during the Civil War – finds the changes he has witnessed in his lifetime unbelievable. He likes to quote one of Spain's better-known poets, Federico García Lorca who was shot in 1936 when he was just 37 years old. The man understood his fellow countrymen well, for his comment that every Spaniard is born with a sign around his neck that says, 'I am going to do exactly as I like' is generally accepted with a wry smile.

Lorca's other oft-quoted remark, that in Spain there is a law for everything but no justice, would not be easy to argue against either.

Another interesting comment on the Spanish character came from a Madrid psychiatrist who was talking on television about new European guidelines as to what constitutes legally certifiable insanity. Referring to his fellow countrymen's trait of doing something they felt like doing with a total disregard for any consequences to everything and everybody else, he said: 'If these regulations were to be applied rigorously, I believe I could certify every person in the country'. It's the sort of statement that could lead to war if a foreign politician came out with it. But he is a Spaniard, too.

The time

Something which can lead to confusion is the difference in time between the United Kingdom and Spain, for in Iberia you are on Central European Time. Anyone who has been to Spain on holiday will know that once the plane lands, you need to move the hands of your watch on an hour. However, when living in Spain you will need to note the dates on which the spring-forward-fall-back adage applies. With the advent of European union, the timing is the same, so you will always be that hour ahead of the folks you have left behind.

If you miss the date though, the sort of muddles that still happen in England can follow you. Like one lady who got the vicar and his wife out of bed at seven o'clock one autumn Sunday morning because she had forgotten to change her clock and thought he was late for 8am Holy Communion. She made up for it the following spring when the faithful were at the communion service. They heard a clattering and cupboard banging coming from the vestry, and all was revealed when she appeared – complete with pinny and bearing a vase of flowers. It was her turn on the flower rosta … and she had not changed her clock again! Or like the British couple who wondered why all the shops in Main Street, Gibraltar, were not open when they rolled up an hour early.

The fixing of time bands across the European Union is currently the subject of review on the part of the European Commission. The result of their deliberations is not yet known but with various parliaments having to pass acts to enforce any change it will be some time yet before anything actually happens. Of course, with the world carrying on turning whatever we do with the clocks, there is the problem that the sun rises over Greece a couple of hours before it is seen in Iberia while some European citizens are 20 degrees further north than those in southern Spain.

The shrug

Something the expatriate will have to become accustomed to is the shrug of the shoulders. It is a gesture of apparent helplessness which says louder than words, 'There is nothing I can do about it'. The man handing out the car parking ticket will do it if you query the charge. The woman behind the supermarket counter will do it if the automatic till breaks down and you have to wait. The town hall staff will do it when you raise a question about anything that is not their direct responsibility …

The difference in attitude which causes the shrug is best explained by the comment of an accountant who was being pestered by a British client as to why he was unable to sort out a problem with the local town hall. 'Why are you in such a hurry to pay?' he asked. 'You British are all alike. You want to pay everything straight away. Why don't you just wait and leave it until you're asked?'

When the man urging him to expedite matters pointed out that if it were left, he might have to pay a further 20 per cent fine for being late, he added, 'But if you wait, they might not send you the bill at all and then you will have gained 100 per cent'.

Spain's difference is something that has to be accepted if you are going to live there. It is their country, they are going to do things their way. You may think you know of a better way of doing things or another answer to a problem. Forget it. 'This is how it is done … our way!'

4 Where to settle

The scale of Spain

All Englishmen know that France is 'different' and that once you cross the Channel life will not be lived the Anglo-Saxon way. Cross the Pyrenees, and there is a further stage of difference. In fact, driving over the mountain range which has acted as a wall to keep the cultures north and south apart throughout history gives a better understanding of how much things change once you have entered Iberia than can ever be gained by flying into a Spanish airport a few hours after leaving home.

The sheer scale of the country is one of the things that impresses anyone driving or taking a train across it for the first time. Instead of a town or village cropping up every few miles in the green countryside, as Britons are used to, the road or train winds over mountains and across vast plains where the pervading colour is brown. Agricultural communities occur now and then, all seeming drab after the be-flowered colour of their French counterparts. The larger cities come almost as a shock in the middle of all this space and emptiness.

Only then can you realise what it means, Spain being four times the size of England, and just what Napoleon and Wellington's men had to contend with when they were marching across this landscape, and why a civil war could take so long to conclude when armies were scattered across this countryside.

It also explains why, with the tourist and expatriate populations clinging to the Mediterranean fringe and leading to all the development there, it is possible to drive inland for under an hour and find enough open space in which to hide an army where you can walk and encounter only a handful of other people all day.

To lump all this together as Spain is misleading. From Galicia and its Atlantic climate in the green and rainy north-west corner, it is a far cry – in more than distance – to the white-walled Moorish pueblos of *Al Andalus*. Indeed one elderly lady, who was proud of her roots in Leon and her Spanish pronunciation, summed up the attitude of many from the north. Asked what she thought of the way the Spaniards in Andalucía run words together in long breath-phrases, like a stick being drawn along a picket fence, she replied, 'They are not Spaniards. They are Moors'.

The Basques, with their own culture overlapping into France, have a separate language and demand that the País Vasco region of the country be called Euskadi.

The proud Catalans, at the other end of the French border, insist on signs being in their own tongue as well as Spanish and that the region be spelled Catalunya and not Cataluña, while to their south Valenciano is taught in the schools and locals speak it to show out-siders they do not have to speak Spanish in the Comunidad Valenciana.

In fact, though Ferdinand and Isabella officially completed the unifica-tion of Spain when they conquered Granada in 1492, there is still evidence of its being a union of separate kingdoms in much the same way that the Scots, Welsh, Irish and English make up the British. The diverse nature of the people known as Spaniards is acknowledged in the way the country is governed, for while international and nationwide matters are dealt with in Madrid, affairs affecting the daily lives of fam-ilies are largely handled by autonomous *juntas* which rule each of the country's 17 regions.

The regions

The regions are Galicia, Asturias, Cantabria, Castilla y Leon, Madrid, Extremadura, Andalucía, Castilla-La Mancha, Murcia, Aragon, La Rioja, País Vasco/Euskadi, Navarra, Cataluña/Catalunya, Comunidad Valenciana, Canarias and Baleares/Balears.

Each of these is responsible for many of the things close to the everyday lives of those living within their borders. This is why essentials such as education, health care, roads and environmental matters are dealt with differently in various parts of the country.

It is also why – with Brussels passing on Europe-wide instructions for implementation, the central government in Madrid enacting laws, and the regions formulating their own policies – it is impossible in a book such as this to lay down hard and fast information that will be current and dependable throughout Spain on many topics. The time and the place may both make a difference as to what is required of the citizen due to the diversity of factors affecting the way in which the structure of Spanish society is built.

Not only may the way in which medical treatment, for example, is provided be different from region to region, but it may change in one of them while remaining the same elsewhere. With individual provinces enacting further legislation within each region and local town halls involved in carrying out much of the detail on the ground, it is easy to see why it is stressed that it is important to check what local requirements and customs apply in the actual area in which you are seeking to settle.

The 17 regions are broken down into a total of 52 provinces, each with its own post code and responsibilities, such as vehicle registration. For instance, the smaller regions of Madrid, Murcia, La Rioja, Navarra and the Balearic Islands are covered by just one post code apiece while a large region like Castilla y Leon is divided into nine provinces.

This diversity of background also explains why the Spanish dialects you will hear vary as much as the English to be encountered in Glasgow, Cardiff or Newcastle.

Coast or countryside?

So, when you aim to retire to Spain, where do you want to settle in this vast and varied land? Most will head for the Mediterranean coast, for it is here that the climate has provided the ideal setting for the holiday industry which has caused foreigners to become acquainted with Spain and get a feel for the land in the first place. It is from these relatively short visits that the desire grows to stay longer and maybe live here permanently. But living somewhere is not the same as being cosseted in a hotel or being able to pop out for a full English breakfast in a café while on a self-catering break. Retiring to the sun means living there for the rest of your life, meeting the bills full-time and not blowing all your money by the end of a fortnight.

Building is going on apace all along the 1,300-kilometre coastal strip from the French border north of Barcelona to Portugal, south of Huelva. Old properties to do up are not generally available though, simply because the whole of this explosion of new development has only recently happened. But there is a huge selection of property on the market. To some extent, the ongoing building boom has prevented prices rocketing as they have in Britain, but they are far from stable.

Popular pockets of foreign residents exist along most of the coast with the Costa del Sol on either side of Málaga and the Costa Blanca around Benidorm being best known. The expatriate enclaves on the Balearic Islands and the Canary Islands must not be ignored either. In these areas it is possible to find a development where most of the residents are British or, at least, English-speaking. Here you can be almost insulated from any involvement in Spanish life at all. On the other hand, there are lots of expatriates whose homes are in either mainly Spanish or multi-national communities. The choice is yours.

The islands

Many who have come to know Spain through holidaying on its islands find they have to make a decision as to whether to live permanently on an island in either the Canaries or Balearics. Large English-speaking communities are to be found on Gran Canaria, Tenerife, Mallorca, Menorca and Ibiza, for example. They prove the ideal spot for some while others get to feel cut off from the mainstream of European life and move to the mainland where they can get in the car and drive 1,000 or 1,500 hundred miles. This is probably a bigger consideration for Dutch, Scandinavian and German pensioners, however, who can drive door to door between two homes or from family to Spain without the added cost of crossing the Channel to contend with. For most Britons, travel is usually by air. But it is something worth considering before making that important decision.

For those who still want to feel near a bit of Britain, the sight of Gibraltar along the coast can be comforting even though it may mean queuing for hours to cross the border to get cheaper fuel and English marmalade. Others, with French links or who aim to drive rather than fly home, find the Costa Brava suits their requirements as it virtually halves the distance to Calais compared with, say, Cadiz.

Wherever you decide to settle, it pays to take a long, hard look at the immediate neighbourhood – not just at what is there, but what could be built nearby. A favourite ploy of developers is to sell apartments or townhouses in a block that has magnificent views to the sea or mountains only for those who have purchased them to discover within a couple of years that the next block is going up plumb in front of their terrace … view gone!

Emily went for a job as a salesperson at one very pleasant apartment complex and, having been hired, was shown around. 'What's that?' she asked pointing out an array of tanks just along the valley below one of the terraces. 'It looks like a sewage plant.'

'It is,' said her new boss. 'Just tell them it's a trout farm'. Emily did not take the job. 'I couldn't do that,' she explained. Someone else could. All the apartments are sold. Before you buy, take a walk round the area in which you intend to live. The sight and scent of effluent may not offend you; on the other hand, it just might.

In some places, narrow roads may be a concern, in others the cheek-by-jowl nature of the buildings may not be to your liking. But it might. Take Nigel and his wife, for example. They found a peaceful Spanish spot which their new neighbours loved. But they had been used to a bustling part of London and hated the silence, what they termed 'the nothingness'. They couldn't sleep at nights with only the occasional tinkling of sheep bells or the odd nightingale song to disturb their slumber. They moved into the middle of a busy tourist town with a road running by their home and have lived there contentedly for years. It just depends what you want.

There are other considerations, too. Some places are dominated by specific nationalities. For example, Torre del Mar between Málaga and Nerja on the Costa del Sol is very popular with the Germans. Restaurant and bar names along the fine promenade give the impression you could be on the Baltic. It could be what you are look-ing for, but it wouldn't suit everybody.

Looking ahead

If you intend looking for a home that is not in the middle of a built-up area it is a good idea to think a few years ahead. Being remote may be fine at 50 but knowing the clinic is not ten miles away could become important later on. And, even if you are in good health, it is handy to have a shop within walking distance for when the car is in the garage.

On the other hand, you may not enjoy being too near some ameni-ties, like the Danish lady who found her dream apartment in a marina complex. It was expensive, but she decided to buy it anyway. Within a few months, however, a nightclub had opened in the space below her which she had assumed would be for further housing. Complaints did no good and, after being woken up at any hour up to half past six in the morning for months, she got out by selling at a loss.

Another amenity that it may be important to take into consideration is an airport. If you are going to be heading back to England at reg-ular intervals, it could be a blessing to have a link to the rest of the world not too far down the road. Airport parking is always on the expensive side and knowing that a taxi won't cost too much or that there is a bus or train connection may be worth thinking about. The same considerations apply even more so if you have friends and family who are likely to come out and visit on a regular basis – and they will! Picking people up at the airport and then returning them in time for their flights can soon become a chore, especially if the round trip involves several hundred kilometres, which it easily might in this larger land.

Train connections may also be something to think about if you intend making use of Spain's good rail system or putting your car on a train to take it to Bilbao for the crossing to Portsmouth, as many do, instead of hitting the road across France.

The proximity of health care has already been mentioned. But if help in the home is required, it is only in municipalities with a population of more than 20,000 that it is a legal requirement for the town hall to ensure care to assist the elderly and infirm is available – although many communities do in fact provide some help. However, it is normally not of the same standard as that expected in the UK and will only be provided for the registered resident.

Sufferers of rheumatic and arthritic aches and pains tend to find the warmer climate eases their condition and some who have trouble with their sinuses also gain relief. However, humidity may be considerable during the winter in some areas where catarrh problems do not go away for everybody. Overall, there is little doubt that the milder climate does make for an improvement in health. The whole issue of health care is looked at in detail in Chapter 12, but whether being on the coast, several hundred feet above sea level or in or out of an urban environment is best, is the sort of personal matter only the pensioner heading south can determine for themselves.

Wherever you do go, however, the cost of eating out will be way below what you have been used to in Britain. Every establishment must put up a list of prices and in areas where expatriates and tourists abound it will normally be in several languages. Among items offered, there may be a *menu del día*, the choice for the day at a modest price. If you don't like cooking, it may pay to look for somewhere that has a choice of restaurants you fancy so you need not worry about wasting away.

5 When to move

Financial considerations

These are probably the most important factors when determining the right time for making a move to any new environment. They are seldom taken in isolation though, and such aspects as family ties, work commitments and the fluctuating price of property all come into play. And behind it all is the weather. Everyone might be planning to retire to the Orkneys instead if they had a climate like southern Spain there!

It is a fact that the weather in Britain affects holiday bookings in Spain. It is taken for granted that all will be set fair for summer on the Mediterranean and the Canaries, but the same certainty of sunshine cannot be relied on by resorts on the North Sea or the Channel. Britain can be beautiful when high summer lives up to its name and after a year when there *is* a summer, the short memory many seem to have entices them to ask, 'Why go abroad?' The following year they book a holiday nearer home. The number of visitors to Spain and other warmer destinations takes a dip.

There is, however, an upsurge in bookings for places abroad that can depend on sunshine if the more normal rain, fog and chill winds have kept bathers off British beaches for the holiday months. Then the number of visitors to Spain increases again. Far more predictable are bookings for long stays in hotels and self-catering apartments during the winter. Folk in Scandinavia, Germany and Britain know their home countries are going to be grey and inhospitable during the dark months, and head south.

It is not surprising that it is towards the end of the year that most expatriates choose to make the move in the same direction. Those who have homes or family with whom they stay in Britain make their way back to their Spanish abode at this time of year, too. Like seaside resorts in the UK, the regular residents find the place comes back to life when the school holidays are over and winter activities begin. The difference is that in Spain, winter is the time when many of the things enjoyed during an English summer come into their own. That is when bowls leagues get into their stride and when cricket teams start the season's fixtures.

Two groups

People making the most of these winter facilities are in two camps: those who live in Spain full-time (though some may spend part of the year in the north) and those whose first home is still in their country of origin but who escape its winter by staying in a holiday home of their own or as long-stay guests in an apartment or a hotel.

The first group are the bridge burners who become Spanish residents and move their lives lock, stock and barrel. Their benefits are not just climatic but financial. For example, when house prices in Britain are rising rapidly and the pound/euro exchange rate is favourable (as in the early years of this century for example) some British folk can create an additional pension fund by selling up and settling in an entirely new location.

The second body of people are even more difficult to quantify than those who make the move permanently, and the only safe figure is to agree that there are many thousands of them. Many of them become part of the scene through their regular visits, staying in the same places even if they stay on a busy winter caravan and camping site, rent accommodation or book a room in a frequently visited hotel. Things they miss include carpets on the floors, but the only moans are usually about the higher price of items like Marmite, tea bags and cornflakes.

If you are one of those planning to visit southern Spain during the winter, do not take only the sort of clothes you would need during a summer vacation. You may need them for sunbathing – and even a dip in the sea in some areas – because there will be days when you can luxuriate in temperatures similar to those of England in July. But there will be wet days as well and within hours of sitting on a flowery terrace enjoying a shirt-sleeve cup of coffee, once the sun dips behind the mountains the temperature can sink to levels that remind you it is still only January.

Many of these over-wintering visitors do eventually become permanent residents as they find their lives more and more fulfilling in Spanish surroundings and as they become more disenchanted with the comparative drabness of life in the colder climes. After all, taking time to find out what living in Spain is really like, as opposed to being a holidaymaker there, is a wise move and some set out on a winter expedition with every intention of settling full-time eventually. Deciding what they want, and then finding it, will largely determine the timing of their migration.

They are among those who have overcome that first obstacle to leaving the UK – the economic one. Some people are able to make the move whenever they feel like it, but the vast majority have to weigh up the financial factors carefully before taking such a dramatic step. A dozen or so years ago it was said that if you had a home and £100,000 in the bank your future in Spain would be secure. With depleted interest rates and costs rising as steeply in the opposite direction, the same scenario will not provide such a happy outlook now. Add a state pension to the equation and things begin to look much more satisfactory, however, and with a company or private pension topping things up as well, the picture is positively rosy. With just the state pension to rely on, budgeting has to be very tight and while some do live in their own apartment with little more in the way of financial backing, there is nothing left over for luxuries and every centimo has to be guarded. It would not take much in the way of a monetary wave to rock the boat, put it in danger and maybe swamp it altogether.

Security

It is this determining of financial security that is the key to the timing of most expatriate arrivals in Spain. With investments accumulated from the sale of companies, golden handshakes, legacies and the like, those who are able to retire in their 50s often make the move before reaching the national retirement age. One young man who was lucky enough to come into a fortune made the move having declared himself retired at the ripe old age of 32! But he is the exception.

Many more feel the lure of Spain as he did, and decide to move there long before they can afford to retire. The lucky ones find work there in their own field while others take redundancy money or a bequest and invest it in a business in an area of which they have grown fond. Often this enterprise is a bar of one sort or another and at any one time there are hundreds if not thousands who are struggling to make a living by catering to tourists passing through or expatriates living nearby.

When hopeful souls with little or no experience of being behind the bar rather than leaning on it have money to invest and ask about buying a bar, sound advice is not necessarily to visit an estate agent but to look around until they find the one they would like to run and then make a bid. It is more than likely that the present owner will be willing to sell. But that is not retiring to Spain. That is taking on a whole new load of long hours and effort. It does not really come within the remit of this book which is to help those who are now looking forward to being waited on, not serving others. It is as well though, to understand how hard some Brits are prepared to work to live in the very place the pensioner can enjoy. It is important to be aware, too, that many less fortunate Brits have lost their shirts in pursuit of the Spanish dream.

Family commitments

Family commitments are also often involved in determining when is the right time to retire to the sun. The proportion of expatriates who have divorced and re-married is relatively large and starting a new life together in a brand new environment where they will be taken on face value with no reference to the past is clearly a factor that goes a long way to encouraging some folk to seek pastures new. After all, if they are going to up-sticks and start again it might as well be somewhere nice.

When to move is so much a personal decision that it is impossible to lay down any hard and fast rules. Knowing the bills will be paid, with a bit left over, and being sure everything will not be compared with what is happening a thousand miles away are probably the two most important ingredients for successful integration, however.

6   *Affording it*

The euro effect

Anyone moving to Spain today with the preconceived idea that it is a cheap place to live will soon be disabused. A couple of decades ago, when the country was emerging from the Franco era and the Common Market had yet to make its presence felt, Spain was lagging behind those in the forefront of Western development. A new materialism has arrived, however; Spain has caught up. While others have dithered, the Spaniards have joined in the European Union with gusto and accepted the euro with open arms.

Those who saw Britain go metric have witnessed the same price-creeping veiled by the arrival of new coinage and paper money which has taken a while to feel 'real'. The building boom and low interest rates have fuelled a leavening in prices across the board, with the result that the cost of living is comparable with the UK. The recent runaway house-price rise in Britain means property is still relatively more reasonable, however, despite a steep upward curve in prices throughout Iberia. Tobacco and alcohol are still cheap with even the French crossing the Pyrenees to stock up. The climate means fuel bills are down for the British, too, and thousands of pounds can be saved by simply buying a new car in Spain rather than in Britain.

The biggest differences in recent years were caused by the value of the euro compared with the pound. At one time, pensioners who were paid in Sterling saw the amount they had to spend leap once it was exchanged for the new currency. This upward trend was well into its stride during the latter days of the peseta with around half as much again the result within a matter of a few years before the 2002 start date for the introduction of the euro arrived. Although the level of the pound relative to the euro is no longer as advantageous as it was, it is still favourable. So the rise in prices has been cushioned for those whose home countries have not arrived in Euroland. The trend for the euro to strengthen, particularly against the US dollar, makes the currency exchange rate something it would be unwise to bank on in the long term.

Of course, the cost of living is lower for those who eat what Spaniards eat and do not insist on a traditional English diet. But let's start with the most necessary item of all, somewhere to live.

House prices

To answer the question of how much a house costs in Spain is like trying to tell someone what a house costs in England … or answer the question, 'How long is a piece of string?' It all depends on what you want and the location. Unless you are seeking something grand, you should be able to find a retirement home and have something left over from what you would get for a similar home in Britain, particularly one in the South East.

There are, of course, prime sites – such as those alongside some of the more prestigious golf courses – where it is easy to face a bill of double what you might expect to pay elsewhere, and there are some where you can pay enough for a site to afford a complete villa anywhere else and still have to sign a contract to pay a minimum of £300,000 for the construction. It depends on what you want and how much you can afford.

If you move out of the touristic, foreign-dominated, holiday and retirement home areas your new home will cost considerably less. In recent years there has been a move inland but amenities are not so readily to hand and unless you have a good grasp of the language, you may feel isolated. In a few years it may be difficult to sustain your lifestyle in a remoter area, but there are some truly remote rural spots for those who seek them.

Rental accommodation is plentiful along the coast, of course. But it is geared to the needs of short-term visitors and can be as pricey as similar housing in Bournemouth or Hastings. Out of season, the prices are lower but it must be remembered that Southern Spain has a protracted season, and those who want to stay for the winter keep letting values high throughout the year. Another problem is that Spanish law makes long-term rental contracts less attractive for the owner. Once someone has a lease for more than eleven months, it can take long, legal wrangles to remove a tenant so it is likely that any long-stay rental will be for renegotiable, short-term duration. And, of course, as property prices rise, so does the amount anyone expects to get back from letting it. Most estate agents will have rental property on their books and English-language newspapers are a good hunting ground for those who want to rent as well as those who are looking to buy. The best advice, whatever type of home you are seeking, is to spend some time in your chosen area, either in a hotel or apartment, and have a good look around. If you can stay an entire winter somewhere, it will improve the odds of your finding exactly what you want and making the most of your money.

The cost of utilities

Once you have found your home, the bills will roll in just as they do in England. Gas is most often delivered in bottles, the hefty orange containers of *butano* being brought to your door for the equivalent of around £6 apiece, though this price may fluctuate. You will need to sign a contract for this service. New, alloy bottles of gas which weigh considerably less are becoming available in many areas, but they require another contract with a different company. Ask around. How you use gas will obviously affect how much it costs to run your appliances but a bottle should last getting on for a month when used for hot water in the bathroom and over the kitchen sink as well as some cooking.

Generally, electricity bills work out as much the same as those in England though you may have to get used to breaks in the supply now and then, especially when the first autumn rains arrive. Like phone bills, they come every two months, not quarterly. Water is a good deal cheaper and, in spite of the hot, dry summers, is not normally affected by hosepipe bans. The huge increase in demand has left some areas wondering where they are going to get enough from, however, especially if another drought occurs like the one in the early Nineties from which ground water levels have not fully recovered.

Telephones

Phone charges used to be considerably dearer but with the growth of mobile phone use, Telefónica, the Spanish phone company, has introduced all sorts of inducements to try and keep its landline market. One useful offer for expatriates is their deal that offers 15 minutes a day between 8pm and 8am throughout the week and all day on Saturdays, Sundays and bank holidays to any on-line phone in the EU. The only charge is €9 (about £6) a month which can mean considerable savings. Telephónica had a monopoly for some 70 years, but now several companies are offering cheap calls to any other country outside Spain once you pay them to rent their prefix numbers. Other firms offer a cheaper service both inside and outside Spain with no initial payment. Of course, you still need a Telefónica line and it depends on your personal requirements – like how many relatives you have in Australia or the United States.

Until mobile phones came along, the state monopoly was in no hurry to install new lines and it regularly took anything from two or three years to get the phone on. Brenda, for instance, had waited years before the men turned up to connect her three-bedroomed villa, and was flabbergasted when they hauled in a switchboard and ten extensions. It was that or go to the end of the queue, they said when she protested. So she had phones in every room (even in the smallest one), and beside the barbeque and the pool all linked through the plug-in control panel in the hall until things were sorted out. Now, however, it is usual for a request to be dealt with and the phone on in a few working days, though there are regional variations.

The ubiquitous mobile phone is in evidence just as it is in the UK with some people apparently unable to shop, eat or even walk without one clamped alongside their head. Several systems with their own cards are available in Spain, and it is a matter of choosing the one that most suits your particular needs as there are several different tariffs available with some parts of the day free on some of them and reduced rate offers on others. It is worth noting, however, that calls from a land line to a mobile phone cost considerably more than those to another land line (although this is not true for mobile to mobile calls). So where someone you are going to call has both, it pays to take the cheapest option.

It is easy for any UK subscriber to fall into another mobile phone trap. If they take their handset with them it will cost the price of an international call every time they talk to someone once they cross the Channel, for instance from their Spanish apartment to a local shop. This is because they will be making use of another company's facilities with the call, in effect, being made on a foreign network, sent to the British system and then back out again.

Another practice which is being looked into is the charging by Spanish mobile companies when their clients receive incoming messages as well as when calls are made. As an example take the case of Harold, a British pensioner who moved into a new apartment and did not think it worth while to have the phone installed. His family, however, bought him a mobile in case of emergencies and put €40 worth of calls on the card. When they checked it a few months later, they found they could not make a call as all his time had expired. He had not made a single call and all the value of his card had been wiped out by his clearing the text messages sent to him by the company itself.

Motoring costs

One area that is definitely more affordable in Spain is motoring. All Spaniards have fallen in love with the car in recent years with the result that the motorist is dealt with more kindly in Spain than in the

UK. All fuel is cheaper, with diesel at around half the UK price. This makes diesel-engined cars popular as the extra mileage is not the only advantage. New car prices are also way down, as are servicing costs. There is no road tax, a cheaper version being administered by each town hall so that the level can be much less in some rural areas than in coastal cities.

Insurance though is dearer than in the UK. A fuller look at motoring in Spain will be found in Chapter 9.

Pensions

So what happens to your pension when you become a Spanish resident? Well, your Retirement Pension remains the same. You will also continue to receive any Bereavement Allowance (payable for a maximum of one year), which used to be called the Widow's Pension, and Widowed Parents' Allowance (which replaces the Widowed Mother's Allowance and is payable to both men and women). Most other benefits will not be paid once you move outside the United Kingdom.

If you are going to be out of the UK for less than three months and you are receiving your pension on a weekly basis, it can be taken as a lump sum on your return or it can be paid direct into your British bank account. However, if your move is permanent, it can be paid directly into a Spanish bank or one in any country which is a member of the European Union. You will also continue to receive any increases in the basic state pension.

Having your pension, either state or private, paid into a Spanish bank is not always a good idea, however. Your local bank should not make a charge for accepting a payment into the account from the UK Department for Work and Pensions, but some do. This is because they normally make a charge on Sterling payments and the commission for this work is the equivalent of around £5 a time. This can be effectively a reduction in your pension every month. The answer is to find a more amenable bank. Or it may be better to have it paid into a Sterling account outside Spain. Many, especially along the Costa del Sol, use Gibraltar banks and building societies for this, mainly because they like to go along every so often and draw cash personally. Banks in the Isle of Man or the Channel Islands, where there is a more developed degree of credit protection, are equally suitable.

With two accounts – one Sterling and the other in euros – it is a matter of a phone call to move your income into the one that holds your 'living' money when the exchange rate is most favourable. You can then transfer funds to your Spanish bank as you need them rather than take whatever exchange rate is applicable on the day your pension is paid in. There may still be a charge, but it can cover a large sum rather than having to shell out for every pension payment you receive. You will, of course, need the Sterling account as well so that your income can flow through it, and it will also be useful whenever you visit the UK and need pounds again. If you are moving permanently to Spain there is no need to keep an account in Britain at all. At the present time, Sterling accounts pay a higher rate of interest than do the euro ones – though it is still not much.

It is worth noting here that if someone gives you a euro cheque, even one on the same bank, there will be a charge when it is paid into your Spanish account. Better to draw the cash from the paying bank if it is nearby. It may not be much of a saving, but it is nice to beat the system!

Benefits

Benefits you cannot usually get once you live abroad are: Disability Living Allowance, Attendance Allowance, Income Support, Carer's Allowance and the Winter Fuel Payment (of which more later). With any of these no longer applicable, a pensioner left with only the basic state pension would find their income substantially reduced, and it would make it hard to pay their way in the modern Spain. However, some of these benefits may be paid if you are abroad temporarily, for instance, on a winter break before making any final move, and there are also transitional provisions for some benefits in some circumstances, so do check with the DWP before you leave.

You should also check with the DWP whether you will be entitled to continue receiving Incapacity Benefit or Severe Disablement Allowance if you move to Spain as this may be possible in some circumstances.

Any local Social Security office will have a copy of the booklet entitled '*Going Abroad and Social Security Benefits*' (it is number GL29) which deals with retirement payments and associated benefits. Another leaflet, number SA29, gives more details specific to Spain. The Pension Service at Newcastle-upon-Tyne will advise if you run into a snag. Their address and details are given in Chapter 16.

Winter Fuel Payment

A major bone of contention in recent years has been the withholding of the Winter Fuel Payment from British pensioners living abroad. Such has been the animosity voiced by those deprived, that the DWP has gone some way towards trying to remedy the situation. The end result has been something of a muddle.

Age Concern has not specifically argued for Winter Fuel Payments to be paid in Spain or other countries.

However, the DWP subsequently apologised when they discovered that the benefit is not being paid to those who left the UK before 1998 or anyone who had not been claiming the benefit before they left. The position is that if you have received the Winter Fuel Payment while residing in the UK and have left since 1998 you are entitled to go on receiving it and to claim for any missing years since you last claimed.

The qualifying period used to be a week in September during which you had to be ordinarily resident in Great Britain or Northern Ireland for at least one day. The Department explained that 'Ordinarily resident means that a person must be normally resident apart from temporary or occasional absences of long or short duration.' And it added, 'Ordinary Residence means residence in a place with some degree of continuity and apart from accidental or temporary absence. Alternatively it might be described as residence according to the way in which a person's life is usually ordered. There is no fixed time limit attached to the term ordinarily resident'. Does that help?

Presumably, if you have been receiving the £200 (or £300 if you are over 80) as part of your pension payments, and then you move to Spain you should continue to receive it. To make sure, there is a special form available from The Pension Service for you to claim it. If you have missed out on winters 1997–98, 1998–99 or 1999–2000 there is another form – this is numbered WFP1 (R) – which should net you the back payments as well.

If you move out of the UK before you are 60 and subsequently become entitled to your state pension, you might find it useful to contact the International Pension Centre, which is part of the Pension Service in Newcastle-upon-Tyne. Their address is given in Chapter 16 and they have a special Winter Fuel Payment Helpline on 0845 915 1515 or on the Internet at www.dwp.gov.uk/winterfuel.

Those UK pensioners still ruled out of receiving this allowance feel strongly that it is something to which they have a justifiable claim. They paid the same during their working lives towards the pension as those still living in the UK. They point to the fact that the Winter Fuel Payment was introduced in the first place as a tacit admission that the pension, as such, is insufficient.

Private pensions

Private pensions can be paid in exactly the same way as the state pension. The difference here is that UK tax will normally be deducted before your monthly cheque is issued. If you are a Spanish resident and paying taxes in Spain, you can insist that your pension be paid without any deduction. This involves a paper chase, but it may be worth it.

In Raymond's case, the lazy clerk of a firm handling the pension fund of the company of which he was a former employee, invented a tax code for him when he became entitled to his pension. This was because, as he was now living abroad, no code existed. Protracted discussions with his former employer, the tax office in the area where he had worked and with the overseas department of the Inland Revenue in Nottingham ensued. Forms in duplicate, for the UK and Spain, had to be filled in and stamped by Raymond's local Spanish tax office (where the tax authority is known as *Hacienda*) before withheld taxes were returned to him and all future pension payments paid gross. All that is obviously only worthwhile if you are already paying taxes in Spain or intend to pay all your dues there.

Taxes – and not paying twice

An agreement on the prevention of fiscal evasion and avoidance of double taxation exists between the two countries that was designed to ensure nobody pays tax twice on the same income – or does not pay any at all. It is just that it is up to the individual to make sure it works and that they are not wrongly taxed. This is an essential area to look at if you receive a pension from the UK Government from time served in the Armed Forces, the Police or the Civil Service, for instance. That will be taxed at source and it is easy to find what is left being taxed again unless *Hacienda* is furnished with the appropriate documents.

There is also in existence an international agreement which was designed to catch out the permanent travellers – those who are not officially registered as living or paying taxes in any country. This says that anyone can be stopped when they are crossing any border within the European Union and asked to produce evidence as to where they are paying income tax. Technically, they can then be held until they have paid whatever taxes the country they are leaving thinks fit. It appears to be a piece of legislation that need not worry the average citizen.

When paying your income tax in Spain it is good to know that there is a level below which no tax return actually has to be made. This threshold is at first sight surprisingly high at 21,000 euros (about £14,500 at the time of going to press). Before you get too excited, as many expatriates have, it is worth noting that the small print in the law on this point says that it only applies if all the income is derived from an occupational pension from one source. So, if you have savings which pay any interest, have a part-time job or a private pension in addition to the state one, you have to make a declaration and pay anyway. It's a nice thought, though.

Spanish pensions

Spanish state pensions are paid to anyone who has contributed to the *Seguridad Social* – which translates easily as the Spanish social security scheme – while working in the country either as an employee or self-employed person. The minimum qualifying period is 15 years, but as any payment to the national insurance scheme in other countries is taken into account, even a few years working in Spain can produce a worthwhile pension. It is paid independently of any UK state pension, for instance, though anyone claiming will have to produce proof of payments made to the Department for Work and Pensions. The Benefits Agency in Newcastle will provide these on request.

The qualifying period for a full pension in Spain is 45 years, one more than in the UK, and any pension will be paid as a proportion of that total. For instance, if a person has worked in Spain for ten years, their pension will be ten forty-fifths of the state pension whereas in England it would be ten forty-fourths. Annual increases due to any rise in the cost of living will automatically be added.

Social security payments are much higher in Spain than in the UK for all registered workers. Currently the payment works out at about £130 per calendar month for self-employed workers and employers are faced with similar payments for their staff members. The amount may be even higher as your earnings rise. However, the benefits for employees are greater, too. Everyone working in Spain is entitled to at least a month's holiday and must be paid an additional month's salary in June and November to help with holiday and Christmas expenses. So to employ someone means paying 14 months' salary for 11 months' work. The state plays fair with this arrangement as well, for pensioners also receive an extra month's money twice a year. The 14 payments instead of 12 take the value of any pension received well beyond that enjoyed by UK pensioners. It is difficult to make accurate comparisons, however, as the pensions received by workers in Spain are based on the amounts contributed by employers and employees according to the earnings received, not one fixed amount paid to each pensioner. In the UK, many financial benefits may be claimed which are unavailable to Spanish pensioners.

Investments and credit cards

Another problem area for many expatriates is what to do with their savings once they move out of the environment with which they are familiar. Money in a building society in England, for instance, has tax deducted at source. Moving it to an offshore branch of the same society, which many of them have, means the rate of interest will be higher. However, it also means that if that society were to issue shares to its customers on a change of status, they won't get any as they are only available to those holding UK accounts. So, they could lose out in that way.

The other thing to consider is whether to keep any savings in Sterling or convert them to euros, the currency in which they will be living. When the exchange rate is in favour of that move, it also has to be borne in mind that the interest rate on euro accounts is a good deal lower, so they will immediately lose in that direction. It can be seen that whatever anyone tries to do, there are always minus points to be considered. Generally, it is wise to consult a financial adviser to see what is available.

Funds galore tempt the investor with offers that make sound sense, and there are others which sound too good to be true and, as the financial world knows, most of them are just that. Many expatriates have lost savings, in some cases all they had, to various companies and individuals who have put high-interest propositions before them. As one knowledgeable American put it, 'People come down here with nobody having any idea of their backgrounds and they can say they were whatever they like. Don't trust any of 'em with a dime'.

That is why it pays to take professional advice before investing and, as for trusting a financial adviser, it is a good idea to ask around and seek guidance from those who have travelled the path before you. For example, setting up a portfolio need not be expensive and you can put just about everything you own into it, apart from property. It is a perfectly legitimate way of protecting your savings from unnecessary tax payments. The fees paid for good financial advice are seldom money wasted. It is impossible to avoid financial risks altogether, but the chances of losing out can be minimised.

Credit cards can be used to advantage – or in a costly way – in Spain as anywhere else. For example, use the wrong one, even one issued by your own Spanish bank, and all you withdraw to live on from their cash point will cost you an additional 2.5 per cent. Talk it over with the bank and use another card, and it costs nothing.

The *Letras* system

One final word on financial matters must be on a Spanish system of hire purchase known as *letras*. This amounts to issuing a series of post-dated cheques. If, for example, you buy a car and decide to pay the difference between what is allowed for your old one as a deposit and the price of the new one over 24 months, you sign a couple of dozen *letras* for so much a month. Trouble can arise if you change banks, however, as Tony discovered.

He bought a new car in this way, but a year down the road the bank muddled up some payments and caused him some totally unrelated problems. So he closed his account and took his business elsewhere, thinking he would have his say when they got in touch with him about the car loan. Instead, he received a visit from some impressive gentlemen from a money-lending firm. You see, the bank did not hold the *letras*. These had been passed on to a debt-collecting company who specialise in this business, the bank having recovered their money straight away by, in effect, selling the debt to this firm. It was they who were now wanting to know why Tony had reneged on the debt for, of course, the cheques they held had bounced. And they were not pleased. Repossession of the car was mentioned. Once he explained, all was well, except that every month until the loan was repaid, he received a visit on the due date when he had to hand over the amount owing, in cash, together with an additional fee to cover the collection.

As he said, 'I was in all sorts of businesses in England and thought I had come across every way I could end up on the wrong side. This sort of thing was what happens to other people, not me! Yet every time I think I have covered all the angles, somebody comes up with something new I'd never thought of.'

He is not alone.

7 Property

The undisclosed mortgage

The idea came to Robin after he had moved to Spain and was living on the coast. He discovered where there was a market for peaches and reasoned that if he could find the right place in the hills, he could live in a lovely spot and the cash from growing peaches would pay for the upward trend of his lifestyle.

He found the land he wanted and the price was much cheaper than he had catered for, so he could buy more of it once he had persuaded some backers to put their money into the scheme as well. Even allowing for some large-scale levelling to be done, the tract of land was a bargain. He knew it was a dry area, but a reservoir some kilometres away could provide all the water he needed – once he had organised a pipeline to his property. The cost of running electricity into the mountains to drive the pumps that would push and pull the life-giving water up the hills was prohibitive. But a liquid gas-powered generator was the answer; it would provide the electricity more cheaply. Everything was going well … if expensively.

After he had bought some peach trees that were available, he discovered that peaches are not simply peaches. There are different varieties, just as there are various sorts of apples, tomatoes, potatoes and pears. Even in Spain, and not far from the Mediterranean coast, there are frost pockets where his blossom could be set back or ruined in the spring. His trees were unsuitable for the site. Burn them, he was advised for he needed the right ones if his crop was not to be literally nipped in the bud.

While he was getting to grips with that, he got a bill from the bank. It was for the payment due on his mortgage. Mortgage?

The bank revealed that the reason his property was such a bargain was that there was not just the one, but several mortgages on the land. As the new owner, he had assumed liability with the purchase and was now responsible for paying them off. Needless to say the local farmers who had sold him the land were unconcerned by his predicament.

It was the end of the money put in by himself and his investors. End of dream.

Normally the deed would contain a clause to state there were no claims against the property. It would appear that in this case, however, no such statement was included.

The worst thing is that this story is not unique. All sorts of hidden pitfalls are found by people buying property, largely because they do not check sufficiently before putting their money down. Buying a retirement home may not lead you into the sort of mess in which Robin found himself, but nobody wants to find themselves in a mess at all, even a relatively simple and less expensive one from which to extricate themselves.

Had Robin gone to the land registry for the area – the *Registro de Propiedad* – they would have had on record just who held the title deeds (the *escritura*). The mortgages would have been revealed.

Buying is easy

To buy property in Spain is all too easy. Mortgages are available, and they are currently cheap even for foreigners should you need one, and once the price is agreed between the current owners and the prospective ones it is simply a matter of fixing an appointment with the *Notario*, who is, in effect, a Commissioner for Oaths, and completing the paperwork. This meeting with the *Notario* is essential and the title deeds which his staff prepare are signed in his presence and he witnesses the transaction. Once his work is complete, you – the new owners – have legally taken over responsibility for any debts or claims against the property.

Normally, all fiscal details are taken care of by the *Notario* and his staff. The prospective buyers must be aware that the various taxes and demands involved in becoming the owners will account for at least an additional 10 per cent on top of the agreed price. For instance, there will be an IVA charge (this is the Spanish equivalent of the familiar VAT) of 7 per cent of the declared value if you buy a new property from a builder or promoter. If a mortgage claim against the property is known about or any taxes are outstanding, he will deduct what is necessary from the money being handed over. There may be a charge for early termination of a mortgage as well, and there will certainly be the fees which the *Notario* will take for his services. These are 0.5 per cent of the value of the property. The estate agent (if one is involved) and any lawyer will have their fees paid out by him as a general rule. Real estate agents' fees vary and may be subject to all sorts of suggested solutions, so be careful and make sure just what you are liable for prior to committing yourself. Solicitors' fees are set at 1 per cent of the value.

Another tax which must be paid on every house transaction is the *retención*. Before it was introduced there was a tendency for some sellers to disappear with the money before all the dues and demands had been met. The result, of course, was that the only person the authorities could claim the taxes from was the buyer and this led to all sorts of arguments. So, enter the *retención* – which does exactly what its name implies. For this withholding tax, the buyer retains 5 per cent of the declared value of the property and discloses it on a form which is filled in when the money is handed over to *Hacienda*, the Spanish tax authority. This form is stamped and copies kept by the buyer and the seller.

The vendors can then make application for the handing over of all or part of the money depending on how many years they have owned the property and the difference in value between what they bought it for and what the value is at the time of the sale. If they purchased the house before the end of 1986 there will be nothing to pay and they will get the whole 5 per cent. Other factors will determine whether they receive all or part of the money, nothing at all, or even have more to pay. If the money is reinvested in other Spanish property it can affect the outcome. Those who decide they may have more to pay tend to sit back and see if they receive a demand from *Hacienda* rather than make application to recover the *retención* only to open a can of worms.

Added Value Tax

Affecting the seller is a further tax which comes into play, the *Plusvalía* (the Added Value Tax). This is due to the local town hall. It varies from district to district and is based on a sliding scale of charges according to the difference in the value of the land – not what has been built on it – since it was purchased by the current seller. However long the land has been owned by the vendor, it is only the last 20 years that will be taken into account for the purpose of assessing this tax. Look out for this tax when you come to buy as it is sometimes listed in the contract as down to the purchaser as part of the deal.

The increased value of a property also affects the seller but not the buyer in the form of Capital Gains Tax which was dealt with in Chapter 1. As was noted there, if the seller is over 65 no payment will be due on the price paid for their home.

With what is left after all these considerations going to the vendor on the completion of the sale, it is clear that if the sellers are not totally honest and do not let on that they still owe the bank, for example, they can walk away without that money being deducted. Guess who becomes liable then! That also goes for any outstanding electricity or phone bills, local council taxes, water charges, community fees ... Just as in Britain, after the agreed exchange date, it is the new owner who must settle the bills so it is important to be certain who is responsible for what and when. It is sensible for the buyer to ask the vendor to produce the most recently paid bills for such items to avoid any problems.

Not involved at the time of purchase, but a tax which must be taken note of by all non-residents is the *Patrimonio*. This is a wealth tax which has to be paid every year to the Spanish tax authorities on the value of all assets in Spain which, of course, includes a holiday house or flat. It varies from place to place and is based on a sliding scale starting at 0.2 per cent, so it seldom amounts to very much. You should also pay a tax of 25 per cent on rental income from a holiday home.

All Spanish taxpayers have to include a nominal amount called *impuestos sobre la renta* as part of their income on their annual tax return. This is a charge on the rental income from their home and is payable even if they live there and do not rent it out. It is to take account of the notional income they could have made if it were let. It is 25 per cent but on only 2 per cent of the *escritura* value or *valor catastral* – whichever is higher – of the property. Technically, either of these percentages may change.

Guidance

With so many unfamiliar taxes and payments involved, it is easy to see why newly-arrived Brits need the services of someone they can trust to guide them through the process. Reliable estate agents more than earn their money and the solicitor's fee can prove a good exchange for sleepless nights. The advice, as ever, is to ask around and see how others have fared. They may have suffered at the hands of some fly-by-night you will avoid, or point out someone who has been solving problems for home buyers for years who has become a dependable friend.

Most deals are straightforward and at least as honest as they would be in the UK. It is, however, up to you to find out. And the *Registro* is one place it definitely pays to check *before* you hand over your money.

It is a good idea to visit the *Registro* immediately after buying the property, too. Changing the name of the owner is vital. You may own what is on it, but the actual land is not officially yours until the fact that you have bought it is registered. That goes for your piece of the property in a block of flats, as well. And the *Notario* does not necessarily do this.

Here is a case in point. A promoter who put together the deal with a builder to erect a block of 24 flats decided to sell them to Germans. He had some knowledge of Germany and the language, and this was his route to make more than he might have got by selling them to local house hunters. The company he formed arranged a couple of weekend trips from Germany to a local hotel when the building was beginning to look in shape and took substantial payments on most, if not all, of the apartments. The sale of the two or three bedroom homes was subsequently completed, the transactions duly notarised and off the happy punters went back to Germany.

When they returned individually for a holiday or to start their new lives in the sun, they found local Spanish families living in them who were surprised to see people with suitcases knocking at their doors. The promoter had headed straight from the 'sale' to the *Registro*, made each apartment his private property rather than belonging to his company, prepared new deeds and then sold the apartments a second time. It was discovered that he is now living in South America.

Make use of the Land Registry or see that your fiscal or legal representative does. If a mortgage is involved on a property in which you are interested you will almost certainly find out because any bank holding the deeds against the repayment will have made sure they can foreclose if they have to.

Booming market

The property market in Spain is flourishing, with many Spaniards now buying second homes while the flow of Brits aiming to retire or enjoy a holiday home in the sun continues. In 2002, for instance, according to the Provincial Association of Constructors and Promoters in Málaga, more than 30,000 properties sold on the Costa del Sol were for what is termed 'residential tourism'. And 34 per cent of them were intended for second homes. The pattern reflects what is happening throughout the tourist areas of Spain including the island provinces.

They estimated that 8 per cent more British clients had bought compared with the year before. The value of the euro for anyone holding pounds was, naturally, a factor. The peseta/pound ratio had fluctuated between 240 and 280 to the pound during the previous decade and in its first year of existence, the euro seemed to settle at a level of a bit better than one and a half to the pound, making prices in Spain very attractive.

At the same time, the number of buyers from Germany dropped by 12 per cent. This was not just due to the slump in their economy, but also had something to do with the coming of the euro. With its introduction in 2002, anyone who had accumulated 'black' money under the floorboards or in the attic had to turn it from marks, francs or pesetas into the new currency. Going to the bank would obviously have involved answering some awkward questions. Anyway, by then banks had been instructed to accept no more than one million pesetas (about £4,000 worth) from a customer on any one day. One chosen method of switching the currency was to buy real estate with it. This swelled the building boom all along the *costas* but, of course, the impetus from this one-off effect was losing momentum throughout 2002. It could also mean that not only had the boost from foreign currency-fuelled investments slowed but that some house buyers were recovering their assets by selling the property to retrieve their now neatly laundered euros.

This was the case where some properties were bought 'off the plan' before a brick had been laid. Making stage payments as construction went ahead, the rising market led to some housing gamblers doubling their outlay without them ever officially owning the property. For on completion they sold on to someone who, taking a liking to the finished home, became the first legal owner. It seems a good idea when such investments pay off but, 'There's many a slip …' as the saying goes and some folk taking a chance on new developments are not so lucky.

No gazumping

One fine thing about buying property in Spain is that you will *not* be gazumped. Once you agree to buy a house or flat, you secure the deal by putting down a deposit which is legally 10 per cent of the purchase price agreed but which, in practice, is usually a nominal amount agreed between the parties. The only way the present owners can back out of the deal – for instance, if they want to take a better offer from somebody else – is to pay you double your deposit back.

If you are going to make 10 per cent of the price of a house, it does soften the blow of not moving in. But it seldom happens. It also means, of course, that if **you** want to back out of the deal – for instance, if you subsequently find you could not get a mortgage after all – your deposit is non returnable. In which case it could be you who loses 10 per cent of the value of the home you had intended to buy.

So make sure the finance is in place before you sign anything.

Pitfalls to avoid

Sometimes people end up having to pay out thousands when they have followed the correct procedures and done everything right. Like a Finnish couple who had owned a house in Spain for years and then decided to move. Bertil was a merchant seaman and when he was on a voyage, often for months at a time, his wife would stay in Spain to avoid the Baltic climate. As retirement neared, however, they decided to sell their home in Finland and settle permanently on the Mediterranean in a new townhouse they fancied that had marvellous views from a nearby hillside. There should also have been around £30,000 worth of cash left over from the sale of their present Spanish home, which would make retirement all the more comfortable.

However, their sale dragged and they eventually had to lower their asking price to a level which meant they made the move without this added cushion. There were 42 houses in the new development but only four of them had been occupied, including Bertil's, when the blow fell. The workers walked off the site because there was so much back pay owing them. The promoter's promises were no longer believed as they knew that only a few of the new houses had been sold. The borrowings from the bank, which had financed the venture, could not be repaid on time either. Once the bank heard the building workers had quit, they foreclosed!

Bertil was faced with a demand from the bank, which had quite legally taken possession of the site. The bank told him he would have to pay again to retain ownership of the house for which he held the deeds, having paid 16 million pesetas. With his wife in tears, Bertil now got involved in the complicated Spanish system of auctions which take place to recover money in cases like this.

All the houses were put up for sale with the money still outstanding to the bank fixed as the reserve price to be recovered. Those who knew the routine advised Bertil not to bid. He didn't … and neither did anybody else. The properties were withdrawn and a new date fixed for the legally required second auction. At this one, the reserve was dropped to 75 per cent of the level that had been demanded at the first one under the laws governing the auctions. Once more, the price was not reached and the properties were withdrawn.

Those familiar with the system were not surprised, for this is what usually happens. Then the date of a third auction was fixed and, at this one, there would be no reserve with the bank having to take whatever was bid. In the meantime, Bertil was offered his home for around 12 million pesetas and accepted the advice to take it.

Fortunately, the value of the property rose once the site was finished by another builder, the remaining houses sold, and the swimming pool, gardens and access road completed. The nice Finnish couple were able to recover their outlay from the sale and are now living in another house (which, not surprisingly, had already been standing for several years when they bought it). But they had had to endure a couple of years of absolute nightmare.

Vanishing view

An English couple whose retirement also ended in legal wrangling, through no fault of their own, had their dream villa built where they had a lovely view across wooded hills to the sea from their front windows. They were well off and to preserve this outlook decided to buy the plot on the other side of the road. This they would turn into a garden and prevent anyone else building there and spoiling the panorama.

When they returned from a visit to England, however, they were greeted by a team of builders at work on a house right opposite them – on their second plot.

Investigation by their lawyer into what was going on revealed that the English couple were not the only ones concerned, for two separate Spaniards had paid for the plot before they bought it. It was discovered that the previous owner had come up with several sets of documents and sold the valuable plot to the three different purchasers before heading for pastures unknown. Sorting that out took years.

More straightforward was the scheme worked out by an American. He was renting an apartment from an Englishman who left him a copy of the deeds to the place so that this pleasant and helpful young man could pay some of the bills for him as part of the contract for his living there.

When he returned, he found someone else had moved in who believed he was the owner. It transpired that the American had copied the deeds, told several people he had to return home in a hurry due to a family bereavement, and 'sold' it at a bargain price to at least two people who thought they were lucky to get such a deal. It ended up with their getting nothing. And the American, who had disappeared taking about £50,000 with him, had gone with no one knowing his whereabouts except that he was probably 'in the States somewhere.'

Your Escritura de Compraventa

The answer is to check, check and then check again before you pay out for any property. And once you have got your *escritura* (the title deeds), keep it somewhere safe and be extremely careful who you let have it in their possession.

And getting that *escritura* is not always easy. A case in point involved a villa which was built for an English couple who paid for everything and moved in. Then they discovered that a mortgage was owed on the land on which their own and a dozen other properties had been built along the road. Until this was paid off, the bank would not release the deeds. With several people concerned, it would take time to sort out the muddle, especially as the promoter had dissolved the company from which they had all bought their homes and was operating under a new name somewhere else.

There was no question of them, or any of their neighbours, not owning their homes so nobody pursued the case with much enthusiasm. It would not be until they wanted to sell, that the non-possession of their deeds could be a problem. As a result, it was nearly 18 *years* before they were able to throw a party to celebrate the fact that they had finally got the *escritura*.

Who owns it?

The inheritance laws of the land (which have been looked at in some detail in Chapter 1) can lead to some complexity, too. A German millionaire found this out when he spotted a semi-derelict little house standing on a knoll looking out on vines and olive trees near a picturesque white-walled village. He saw the potential and made enquiries as to who owned it. It transpired that when the old man, who had raised his family there, had died a few years before, his widow and several children had each received their share of the property.

When his widow passed on, a brother had inherited part of her part of the premises. He, too, had died and his widow and children came in for a share. One of the original owner's children had also died and left their share between their offspring. All told, 17 people now had a say in the disposal of the property.

Then there had been a big family row which had resulted in there being two distinct factions within the clan. Though the German had asked them to name their price so that they could all have done very well by splitting the proceeds, because one faction agreed to sell, the other would have nothing to do with the deal. The little house still stands neglected with several other people, besides the German, having given up and walked away.

Another common occurrence is where the titleholder of a property is registered as owning the plot but there is no building listed as being on it. However, if there are complaints about what you have on the land in the way of construction, you could legally be asked by the local authority to alter it, move it within your bound-aries or knock it down altogether because it is not registered as *there* at all.

As a pointer to how careful any buyer should be, an aerial survey of just one coastal municipality a few years ago revealed that there were at least *2,000* buildings – ranging from conservatories, garages and outhouses to complete villas – for which no plans or building permits existed in the surveyor's department at the town hall.

Rustic or urban?

Again, it is best to make sure just what you have on your deeds before you take over as owner of the property. This is particularly important in rural areas where the property will be classed as *rustica* rather than *urbana*. In such places it is legal to add on to the home as the family increases, but it would still be wise to seek planning permission for any construction you plan yourself.

In rural areas, as well as along already existing roads, most con-struction tends to be on an individual basis rather than as part of an entire development. This means it will not be part of a community, the commensurate fees of which we will look at below.

If your intention is to move into rural Spain, several things must be taken into account. Access is important, for many little white houses with fantastic views are approached along unmade tracks that are just dusty in summer but which may wash out and become impassable when rain deluges the mountains in winter. Any bus service is liable to be rudimentary at best and what about shopping – or a clinic if somebody breaks an ankle?

A French couple bought a house in a rural area which had a private dirt lane leading to their land. They used to drive in and park their car under some trees just outside their property, until the Frenchman was rude one day to the owner of the spot where they parked. He then refused them permission to leave their car there though he could not refuse them the right to walk to their property. The Frenchman sued but lost the case. Before they had bought, no one had warned them of possible restrictions on bringing their car in – that is, if they did not have *servidumbre de paso*. In Spain there is a national law, *la Ley de Suelo de España*, which covers the use of the land, but each community and region has its own rules on certain activities. These rules may be changed when a new administration is voted in.

It is unlikely mains water will be available to the majority of rustic premises, so finding out about any well and its propensity to dry up in August is vital. Some people do not mind fetching their water by bottle from the nearest village. Would you? A common phrase in advertisements for rural homes is 'Electricity available'. It may be, but how much will it cost to connect? The chances are that if it would be cheap, it would have been connected already. Take your time and find out first unless you are a real adventurer who loves rising to an unforeseen challenge.

Incidentally, those moving back into the hills often find that several of their Spanish neighbours are only around at weekends. They live and work in a nearby town or city and bring the family to the country to look after the fruit trees on high days and holidays as a total break from urban living, cash from the crop paying for their second home. As Sunday is *domingo* in Spain they are referred to by the charming name of *domingeros*.

Community fees

Payments in the nature of rates on your property will be due to the local town hall and these are detailed in the next chapter (Chapter 8). There will probably be community fees in addition, because such things as roads and sewers on the majority of urban developments in Spain are not always taken over by the council on completion as is the normal case in the UK. The upkeep of such amenities as the sewers, roads and footpaths, street lighting, gardens and possibly a shared swimming pool is therefore an on-going charge which is the responsibility of, and paid for by, owners of property on the development under the Law of Horizontal Property. This was designed to cover the needs of apartments in blocks where, of course, things which are common property like stairs, lifts and the exterior of the building itself have to be maintained at a shared cost. However, the law has been used to cater for common amenities on much larger developments, and rows of townhouses and villas on individual plots are usually part of an urbanisation (the same word is used – *urbanización*) or what in Britain would be called an estate.

Some local authorities are willing to take over the provision and maintenance of some amenities from communities in their munici-palities, sometimes after they have been in existence for several years. But there will still be things like the pool and gardens left for property owners to arrange to look after as councils are not going to accept responsibility for everything. For the majority of expatri-ates, community fees are likely to have to be considered as part of the charge on a property.

Communities can be helpful, but they can also be a source of more discontent than pleasure. With a little give and take, the neighbourli-ness they invoke can produce benefits all round. However, as in anything where everyone has to put money in, people are liable to have differing opinions as to how it ought to be spent, and priority as to what is for the good of the community is not always some-thing on which there is agreement. An example might well be a tennis court, the building of which several residents suggest as they think it would be a good thing to have on part of the urbanisation's open space. It would enhance the value of all the properties, they argue, while a charge for using it would make the scheme self-funding. Others might voice their view that the money would be better used to provide a children's play area. And just where either addition ought to be sited would cause concern for those who would have no objection to either of them a hundred metres away but do not fancy the plink-plonk of ball on racquet or the screaming of children right outside their window.

Swimming pools are something many communities provide and their use is covered by a whole set of rules and regulations. Officially, they must be fenced to prevent accidental drowning; there must be access for wheelchairs or an ambulance gurney; tiled stairs must be provided for ease of entry to the water and not just metal steps; there must be toilet facilities and changing rooms; and in certain circum-stances a paid and certificated lifeguard must be in attendance. A blind eye is often turned on some of these conditions to make it viable to have a pool open at all. But, even then, it is often found that with chemicals and cleaning and water charges the upkeep of the pool is far and away the dearest item on the accounts. Having one handy in a warm climate does, however, add value to all the properties for which it is available.

The only item that normally rivals pool costs in the community bud-get is the cost of administration. There is only one official that a community must have – a president. On smaller ones, if this person is willing and capable, they will often handle the correspondence, pay bills and collect fees as well as see whatever needs doing gets done. This saves an awful lot of money. It is more usual to have a paid *administrador*, however, who has to be a member of the prop-er professional body (the *colegio*), and to their much enlarged emolument must be added the cost of the paid help which will be considerably dearer than when gardens and pool were cared for by the owners themselves or by casual labour.

Once a year every urbanisation, which may also be called a *con-junto* or *comunidad*, has to have an annual meeting. At this, any property owner can put anything they like on the agenda by notifying the president in writing in advance. On most occasions, the accounts are dealt with, which includes fixing the fee payable, and decisions are taken on recovering unpaid fees, appointing officials and electing a president and committee. Any new projects should be decided on for, technically, unless a majority of those paying give their approval, nothing that involves capital outlay should be undertaken unless a separate meeting is called specially to seek official sanction. 'Technically' is the word', though, for many matters are simply carried out by the president and/or committee members as they come to notice.

Who wants to be president?

The position of president is an interesting one for this person is responsible under the law for the operation of all community matters. Only an owner can become president by a straightforward majority vote, and any one of them can be elected whether or not they are a Spanish resident. Usually someone who lives all-year-round on the development takes on the job, most often with the support of a small committee and the advice of the administrator. If nobody will take the position, however, provision is made for the names of all owners – both of them if it is a jointly owned home – to go into a hat at the local town hall where the mayor will draw one. Whoever's name comes out becomes president for 12 months, like it or not. It rarely happens, but it could!

A problem that varies enormously is the level of unpaid fees, with some communities having operated with millions of pesetas outstanding for years. The law was amended a few years ago, however, and the recovery of bad debts is now a much simpler, cheaper and quicker matter. Anyone whose fees have not been paid within 12 months may have an embargo placed on their property by an application to the local court. If the amount is not handed over in full to the court, the property is then sold. The outstanding debt is paid to the community and the rest – less legal costs – handed over to the former owner. Not surprisingly, the level of debt has dropped considerably.

In many instances, contributions towards the upkeep of the community are equally divided between the number of dwellings involved. In some apartment blocks, however, the fee payable may depend on how many bedrooms each proprietor has with a studio owner paying less than someone with three bedrooms, for example. Some larger urbanisations are constituted so that payment is per square metre – the bigger the plot, the more the owner pays. Find out what the rules are, for they could stipulate what colour your home has to be painted or what sort of sunblind is allowed. It is not normally a problem but it is best to know what restrictions apply. Those who fall foul of such regulations are usually owners who let their property become an eyesore simply by not maintaining it. There is usually a way in which the community can put things right and then present the offender with a bill for the work.

It depends how your urbanisation is organised as to whether you can pay community fees by direct debit or not. However you pay, it is essential to make sure that somebody is looking after your affairs whenever you are not in the property whether or not it is on an urbanisation.

Maintenance

That does not only apply to the payment of fees, but the maintenance of the property. If you have a garden, it will need watering and the growth of some of the more virile plants cutting back. One Swedish family arrived on holiday, having made no provision for anyone to tend their house, to find they could not get into the door as the bougainvillea next to it had performed a Sleeping Beauty Castle operation and completely blocked it. They even had a creeper that was cutting out all light in the lounge entwined with the grill on an *upstairs* window.

The community had a gardener who would have kept it tidy for a few euros a week. As it was, the bill for sorting out the small bed beside the terrace – and for carting away the best part of a ton of undergrowth – cost considerably more. You have been warned!

Ask around before employing anyone to carry out maintenance or alterations to your home. There are craftsmen and cowboys in

Spain like everywhere else, and quality of workmanship and prices fluctuate dramatically. Those who enjoy a bit of DIY will find everything they need to hand in the local hardware store, *la ferretería*. A plethora of paints and varnishes is available, mostly of makes unheard of in the UK but almost all satisfactory. Take your dictionary along and make a language lesson out of reading labels on the tins. In any case, the person behind the counter will always advise once he knows what you want it for.

The cheapest way of whitening a wall is with old-fashioned *cal*. This is whitewash – chalk – and locals still make it from lumps of lime mixed with water. If you try it, wear goggles and gloves, and use a metal tub for you would not be the first to see a plastic container melt from the heat generated and the corrosive liquid escape. Any oil – mineral or vegetable – added in tiny quantities to the *cal* will make it last longer. Nothing looks more startlingly white but it will wash off during winter's storms, which is why Moorish villages used to get a fresh coat every May and (in the Balearics, at least) all house interiors were whitewashed annually by the women. Now, plastic-based emulsions are more durable and worth the extra cost, which is not excessive.

Builders' merchants stock all the cement, sand, blocks and bricks you may need. The bricks, however, will not be solid Flettons but hollow *bloques*. Though the dictionary will tell you a brick is *un ladrillo*, that tends to cover facing bricks not the sort walls to be rendered and then painted white are built from. Plastering is done with *yeso*, a powder that has much in common with plaster of Paris. It can set like a rock while still being mixed in the bucket and is not recommended for the novice with a trowel. Timber stores have all manner of material, much of which is just as baffling for the amateur as is the choice in the larger DIY outfits in the UK. All wood, however, is much dearer in Spain.

Much cheaper is the wonderful array of tiles (*azulejos* as opposed to *tejadas*, which are roof tiles). Anyone who has turned their hand to doing their own decorating in the UK will be drawn to the way a home can be beautified, inside or out, with this artistry. After all, tiles and the Mediterranean have been synonymous for centuries.

If you intend to make any additions or structural changes to your house, however, it is important to be sure that you (or your builder) get permission from the town hall. Also, your local council may have regulations covering the exterior of your house – for example, relating to the colour of your shutters.

Owning a hotel suite

Besides villas and apartments, there is another option for housing, and one which several find suitable, especially if they live alone. This is to buy a hotel room. Several hotels do set aside rooms for full-time residents. What is offered is usually a bedroom with bathroom *en suite*, cupboard space, a small kitchen and sometimes a lounge with a balcony; in reality a modest hotel suite. The price usually works out at about the same as a studio in an apartment block. Management fees will probably be higher but there is always the hotel maintenance staff to call on, the hotel's entertainment and dining facilities to enjoy, plus a degree of security provided by the reception desk. On the downside, there will be the normal hotel noises emanating from guests whose hours may be different from your own.

Time-share or, as some prefer to call it 'holiday ownership', is not really a practical proposition for those intending to retire either part-time or permanently. It has become a significant part of the Spanish holiday mix and does provide a means for holiday stays which some folk find suits their needs. One obvious advantage over owning an individual property is that it removes any maintenance problems. It also offers the chance to exchange your period of tenure in an apartment with someone in a different part of the globe. But, if the intention is to return to the same area for more than a couple of weeks a year, to settle even if only temporarily, the maintenance costs alone begin to make this impractical.

Seeking insurance cover for your property and contents obviously applies in Spain just as it does in the UK. It will often be possible to use the Spanish branches of the multinational firm you are already accustomed to dealing with.

8 Town halls and taxes

Rates – *IBI* and *Basura*

Elizabeth knew what it was before she opened the letter from the Town Hall that was among the correspondence waiting when she returned from her stay with family in the United Kingdom. It would be the demand for the rates – the *Impuesto sobre bienes inmuebles de naturalesa urbana*, known to all and sundry as the *IBI*, which was the local tax that had replaced the old *Urbana* a few years previously. She had plenty of time to pay as the period for payment did not end until November.

What she found, however, was a demand for the *IBI* plus a 20 per cent *tipo*, an increment which was the equivalent to a fine, for not paying by the deadline. She was annoyed to find that this year the final date for payment had been moved to 20 September. An angry visit to the *Ayuntamiento* (the Town Hall) next morning taught her it was not up to them to tell her the new date or even send out a bill. In Spain the onus is on the individual to find out when things like car tax, council taxes and the payment for rubbish collection are due to be paid. If the council sends out reminders, as most do, it is their way of helping people. They don't legally have to.

Elizabeth was one of many – and not all expatriates either – who missed the deadline that year. The date had been moved forward in what was seen by many as a crafty means of raising the council a lot of extra money. By pulling in the rates earlier they also eased the loan burden at the end of the financial year. They had saved more money by not sending out reminders, which pretty well ensured they would also gather in all those extra 20 per cents.

The solution was to take out a standing order with the local bank so that they paid demands from the Town Hall whenever they were due. End of problem.

But not for Henry! He had organised direct payments through the bank and was unworried when the notification that he and his wife had paid the *IBI* and their *Basura* – the rubbish collection charge – arrived. Then he found a third receipt. It was for the rates on an apartment they had sold when moving to their present home *14 years before*.

They had heard nothing about the property since, but now here was this notification of payment by their bank out of their account. Henry discovered that the couple they had sold to had, in turn, sold it to someone else the year before. Over the years the couple Henry and his wife had sold to had paid the outgoings, but the new owners had not done so. The Town Hall found that, though the deeds had been in order, no change of proprietor had been made at the Land Registry office. So Henry and his wife still legally owned part of the land the block stood on, and the local authority had simply taken the money out of Henry's bank account.

A trip to the Registry to change the ownership, which cost only a few euros and was soon completed when their deeds noting the sale were produced, meant that the Town Hall were bound to admit their error and give Henry his cash back. This of course took months to arrive back in his bank account as town halls do not pay anything promptly – and they don't pay *tipos* like they levy on everybody else.

Car tax

Something else which your Spanish Town Hall will collect is the car tax you will have to pay each year. With the impressive title of *Impuesto sobre vehiculos de tracción mecánica*, but known as the *Matriculacion*, the amount varies from place to place with the charge likely to be less in rural areas than it is in cities and on the coast. It will also cost more for a high-performance vehicle than it will for a shopping runabout.

It normally falls due in the spring and the town hall will probably notify you before the deadline. But they don't have to – and not all do – so it is a good idea to have a standing order for that as well.

Remember, too, that every owner is legally bound to have an agent representing them when they are absent from their property. A friend or neighbour keeping an eye on things is fine, but somebody should be responsible in your absence as there is no liability on anybody to forward anything to another address; authorities are entitled to assume that once a notice or demand for payment arrives at your address, you have received it. It is up to you to see that it is dealt with on time.

Paying directly through a bank may be safest, but keep an eye on just what is taken from your account. That goes for your electricity, telephone and water bills, too. Spanish banks and their computers are not infallible, any more than they are in the UK.

Empadronamiento – the right to vote

The Town Hall is also the place where you can be put on the census and the electoral roll – *empadronamiento*.

Advice from British Consular officials in Spain is to get your *Tarjeta de residente comunitario*, popularly known as a *residencia* (as explained in Chapter 2), and become *empadronado*. You will then be treated more or less like a Spaniard. People moving to reside or retire to Spain on a permanent basis should, at the very least, register with the local municipality. This is not the same as having your *residencia* and not as onerous. It puts you on the electoral roll so that you can actually vote, but only in municipal and European Parliament elections. But the greatest advantage is that the local authority can get benefits from the regional government to pay for the services it has to provide.

It is extremely unfair that some districts can have a large foreign population, the members of which have not bothered with this *empadronamiento*. They will still expect the local town hall to provide services and grumble if they are not there though the district is not receiving the grants for which it should be eligible. For example, more than 60 per cent of the property within the boundaries of Mijas on the Costa del Sol is owned by foreigners, many of whom are either not full-time residents or simply have not bothered to register. Every owner who has not registered is depriving the town hall of funds in the form of central or regional government grants.

The fact of registering helps the area because grants either direct from central Government or via the regional authority are calculated on a per capita basis. If you are not on the register, the local council does not receive its quota for you. You are paying rates, so why not make more funds available to pay for the good of your community by being on the list?

It is simply a matter of going along and proving you are either the owner or, with a rental contract, are the person permanently resident at your address. You do not have to have a *residencia*, all you have to show is proof of who you are, like producing your passport, and a copy of your title deeds or land registry record to let the council know you own the property. It gets the grant and, come election time, you become a Spanish voter. And that can be an interesting experience, too. Unlike UK citizens, Spaniards did not get to vote freely until the 1970s. Under Franco people could – and in fact had to – vote, but not freely. Politics was a dangerous business. People opposed to his regime had no way of expressing themselves through the ballot box as the ballots were not secret, and to be a Communist or supporter of the Left could lead to imprisonment. Memories of the Civil War and a knock on the door in the night were still vivid in many minds. It was 1977 before secret ballots were introduced, and at that time no one under the age of 62 had ever voted in a free election.

So when the population was enfranchised, many voted for left wing local authorities, more for the sake of proving to their own satisfaction that they could do so without punishment than because they believed in any particular socialist policy.

Proportional representation

Proportional representation (PR) is the way elections are decided in Spain, with the number of seats being divided among the competing parties according to the share of the total vote each of them receives. The number of seats on each local council depends on the number of registered voters, and enough expatriates live in many coastal areas for the number of councillors to be affected by how many of them bother to register and vote. This *empadronamiento* makes them a real part of their new community with a voice as well as an economic presence.

For example, the provinces of Alicante and Málaga – the centres of the Costa Blanca and the Costa del Sol respectively – have more than 65,000 expatriates each who are officially registered to vote. This means that not only is all that extra grant money available to councils, but there are additional councillors serving the population as well, for the population is recognised as being that much greater.

The way the law is established sets down that in each municipality the number of councillors per head of the population will be as follows:

Residents	Councillors
Up to 250	5
From 251 to 1000	7
From 1001 to 2000	9
From 2001 to 5000	11
From 5001 to 10,000	13
From 10,001 to 20,000	17
From 20,001 to 50,000	21
From 50,001 to 100,000	25

A city with more than 100,001 residents has an additional councillor for every extra 100,000 people or part thereof.

How important your vote is clearly depends on how big the place is in which you live. If your home is in a small village, each of the five councillors will represent only 40 or 50 of the inhabitants; if you are in a major city an extra five councillors may be elected to look after the interests of half a million people.

Party lists

Unlike the British system where you can vote for an individual, the voter puts the ballot of the party he or she selects into the envelope with the party designation, and puts this into the ballot box. For example, in a town of 30,000 people each party will list its 21 candidates on the voting paper. This virtually ensures no flippant attempts are made to get on the council.

The candidates leading the parties and hoping to become mayor will obviously be at the top of each list so that they are most likely to be voted on, while those at numbers 17 to 21 will stand little chance of actually becoming a councillor. That is, unless there is a dramatic landslide, or only one group puts forward nominations.

Normally, there will be lists of candidates from the main Spanish political parties as well as groups representing regional or even independent local interests. Whatever the size of the community, to be represented on the council any group must secure at least 5 per cent of the votes. Then the number of seats – in our example 21 – is shared out according to the votes each party receives. If the party is lucky enough to be well supported and receive more than half the votes, it will gain at least 11 places. This will give it an overall majority for the next four years, the term of office.

Often this does not happen under the Proportional Representation system of sharing out the seats which means that a coalition has to be formed so that the work of the town hall can go ahead. To secure this, all sorts of promises have to be given and compromises made, and some of the deals that are done are difficult to comprehend. What might well be looked at askance in Britain seems to keep things working relatively smoothly south of the Pyrenees.

If you are entitled to vote, you are also eligible to stand for election, and a few foreigners have appeared on local election tickets. Most have not actually served as councillors, however, just as the vast majority of candidates will know they have no real chance of being elected when they allow their names to go forward. As in the UK, most of the politicians will seek your advice as well as support in the lead-up to polling day and then be difficult to contact if you have a matter you wish to raise during the next three and a half years.

Do not wait until elections are due, normally in May, as the voting lists will close anything up to four months beforehand. Those who register after the deadline will have to wait another four years. And the sooner you become *empadronamiento* the sooner the town hall will receive some financial benefit from the fact that you live there. You do not just get the right to vote either. Being officially on the census of residents means you are entitled to receive help from council welfare facilities, such as home helps, and to make use of libraries and sports amenities, as well as send children to the local schools if you have any living with you for whom you are responsible.

The Ombudsman

The Spanish government system incorporates an Ombudsman – someone to whom the citizen may complain if they feel that they are being treated unfairly – as is the case throughout the European Union. With the glorious title of *Defensor del Pueblo* (literally the Defender of the People), these representatives of Regional government can literally stick their nose in anywhere if they consider it would serve the best interests of the populace at large. They can also be called on to arbitrate in disputes such as planning permissions that cannot be resolved between local and provincial authorities within their area. However, their conclusions are recommendations and are not necessarily enforceable.

It generally transpires that, when faced with a complaint about a civic authority, they act more as apologists. Most issues that trigger public anger against officialdom occur again and again and these are usually dealt with by the despatch of a routine letter offering long explanations concerning the law which has permitted whatever is being complained of to be a perfectly legal activity.

One regular 'moan' features councils waiting years before claiming overdue taxes so that the amount is increased by fines and then compounded until it is large enough for the recipient of their demand to be liable to have their house, their bank account and anything else of value embargoed until the debt is paid.

9 Motoring matters

Importation problems

Cars and their importation, purchase and registration probably lead to more sleepless nights for folk from other countries deciding to settle in Spain than any other single cause. They certainly create a great deal of work for British consul officials who are drawn into the picture because of a piece of paper which we can't produce.

All Spaniards are *empadronamiento*, an imposing word encountered in Chapter 8 for being registered at your local town hall. Once you are old enough to vote it also means that you are on the electoral roll, just as you would be in the UK. However, with government grants being handed out according to the number of residents in each municipality, local authorities are keen to see that if you move from one town to another, you are removed from the old list and placed on the new one.

The difference in attitudes to registration in Britain and in Spain can cause problems with the importation of vehicles into Spain. This is because the UK citizen has no proof that he actually left there on a given date and the Spanish authorities require this proof. Your car must be registered in Spain within a specified period and the Briton cannot show a document to say when he got there. So, he has to present himself at a British consulate and swear an oath that he left the UK on a specific date.

The consular staff have no way of verifying what they are told, of course, and simply provide the necessary paperwork to satisfy the Spanish traffic department involved. That is the legal way of moving a UK vehicle into Spain.

If you decide to import a vehicle into Spain, you must also show that it has been used in the UK by you for at least six months (in fact, that it is your car and not one you have brought into the country just to pass on to somebody else).

It also has to be shown that it is no longer registered in the UK. This is achieved by obtaining a certificate from the Department of Vehicle Licensing in Swansea. Then you have to show that the vehicle conforms to UK legal requirements such as fuel emissions and seat belts. This is normally straightforward, but it can be a tricky operation. For example, taking in a car made in the United States can cause headaches. If it was bought in the United Kingdom, it is likely that it meets European Union specifications. But, if it has been brought over from the United States and was not originally intended for the European market, further problems arise.

Ask an expert

Dealing with cars and their movement from one jurisdiction's plates on to another's is an area where the advice of an expert can save months of frustration – and, ultimately, expense. In general, the importation of vehicles into Spain is so fraught with obstacles that the advice from British consular officials in Spain is to seek the help of a *gestor* (that peculiarly Spanish official who is best described as somewhere between an accountant and a lawyer) and not to try it yourself.

Unless you have a special affinity with a particular vehicle, by far the easiest solution is to buy locally once you arrive. To own a vehicle on Spanish plates, however, you should be a Spanish resident. You will need your *residencia* for this, but papers to show you have applied for one will suffice, so you do not have to be without a car while the formalities are dealt with. In some places in Spain, an NIE seems to be sufficient.

In any case, the price of cars is cheaper in Spain than in the UK and, in the long run, this is likely to mean considerable savings. Dealers will also sort out all the paperwork for you, and this can smooth the way into the Spanish scheme of things vehicular. Just as in Britain, there are some very good deals available if you are prepared to be a bit flexible in your choice of transport.

When the prices of new cars are down (as in 2002–03, for example), there is not the same gap between the cost of a new and a well-kept second-hand model. If you do buy a used car, be even more careful than you would have been when doing a similar deal before you headed south. Maintenance is not high on the list of priorities for many Spanish drivers.

Having a car thoroughly checked is always a wise move but one thing you are not so likely to find a problem in your new home is rust. With the climate so much milder, any second-hand vehicle is not likely to have encountered the salt which is scattered so liberally on UK highways during the winter and which leads to so much body rot. If you live near the sea, of course, there can be rust damage.

Whether new or used, you will find a larger proportion of diesel engines in Spanish vehicles. Although the cost of fuel overall is well down on what you have been paying, a diesel-engined vehicle may be worth the extra as the fuel is around half the price of that in the UK. It depends on your mileage really as to whether it is worth the additional initial outlay.

Garage bills are generally less than would be regarded as normal in Britain but, as the world over, there are huge variations. Before having any work done, ask for a quote. And, unless it is urgent, ask around and find out where those who have been driving in Spain for a few years go themselves.

For those who feel happier having assistance available, the RACE (Royal Automobile Club de España) fulfils the duties of the similarly organised AA and RAC in Britain. This organisation's number is in every telephone book and most garages will point you in their direction if asked.

Insurance

While most motoring comes out on the right side when compared with the UK, one area where you are likely to find it more expensive is insurance. Premiums are well up and there are not the same reductions and offers to entice long-term, proven-safe drivers as in the UK, though some insurers are beginning to make special offers. This is partly due to the car, rather than the driver, being insured under Spanish law. And should you be one of the many motor caravan owners, you will find that you do not have the same brokerages tempting you with offers any more. There is no specific category for what the Americans call recreational vehicles in Spain and your camper will be rated as a van and hit with the same sort of charges as are paid by a builder whose truck is running around the roads all year instead of just catering for holiday rides. Third party insurance is compulsory.

You may not insure a Spanish registered vehicle anywhere else either. Under European regulations this is no longer permitted. It stems from cross-border scams that were perpetrated in the early days of the Common Market when cars were 'stolen' in one country to be paid for by an insurance company before they surfaced somewhere else only to be 'stolen' and paid for all over again. Not unnaturally, the insurance companies did not like it, so your car must be insured in Spain unless you keep it on British plates and only have it in Spain officially for short periods.

The Spanish attitude to these matters is perhaps best exemplified by the fact that when serious flooding occurred several winters ago, it was discovered that 70 per cent of the vehicles affected by mud and water carried no insurance at all. This lack of cover is not to be recommended, however, for should you have a serious happening, you could end up in gaol thinking how happy you would be to pay many times the premium just to get out.

Two of each

A few other points worth noting are as follows.

Warning triangles

All vehicles on Spanish roads must carry *two* warning triangles. The argument is that on roads other than dual carriageways, it is safer if one is placed a distance of 70 metres in front of any vehicle obstructing the highway as well as the one a minimum of 70 metres behind it. When the law was introduced – according to many wags because someone in the Ministry of Transport had a relative with a factory making reflecting triangles – a flood of cheap warning signs appeared. The law has consequently been amended so that only those which conform to EU standards and are stamped with the appropriate number are legal. This official number is E13 27 R03 0002.

Mirrors

There must always be at least two unobstructed rear-view mirrors on your car. Not being aware of this caused a problem for a driver who had a load blocking the interior mirror in an estate car and only one wing mirror. A second wing mirror on the passenger side would have cost less than the on-the-spot fine when he was pulled over by an observant policeman.

Glasses

Spectacles are something else you may need to have two of as well. If you normally wear them for driving, and your licence indicates this, Spanish law says there must be a second pair in the vehicle with you at all times. If you are stopped while wearing glasses and cannot produce this back-up pair, you may be subjected to an on-the-spot fine. The law was intended to make sure that, should you lose the first pair, you will still be able to see properly. Obviously, if you have lost the first pair and are wearing the replacement ones, you will not have the required second pair with you. A receipt from an optician to show you do own two pairs would presumably save you from the penalty of the law.

Drink driving laws

Do not imagine that because alcohol is cheaper in Spain the drinking and driving law is any slacker than in places where it costs more to overstep the limit. The legal level was halved a few years back, and police are just as aware in Spain that drink is a major contributory factor to many serious accidents. The amount of alcohol in your blood beyond which drivers are likely to be prosecuted is 0.5 grams per litre. The level that applies in breath tests, which are conducted by the *Guardia Civil* purely randomly by the roadside in many areas, is 0.25 milligrams in the air a driver blows into the machine.

If you are stopped, do not argue even if you never touch alcohol. The law requires that you must co-operate and refusing is regarded as seriously as drinking and driving. If your first blow proves positive, you will be given a second test within ten minutes using a more accurate machine which is ominously called an *evidencial*. If that is also positive, your vehicle will be immobilised, and the police will phone a taxi or a friend to take you away. You cannot return to pick up your car until you have taken a further test to prove you are no longer intoxicated. Then the fines and bans will come into effect.

The only safe route is to follow the rule of not drinking and driving. A factor that can help here is that taxis are cheaper in Spain, too. Most rules and regulations boil down to plain common sense in Spain just as they do anywhere.

MOT becomes *ITV*

Your MOT becomes an ITV in Spain (which is nothing to do with television). In most parts of the country you are informed when it is due on any Spanish-registered vehicle, usually once the car is more than four years old, though it varies with commercial vehicles. When notified you must take it – or have someone take it for you – to a registered test centre. No garages are registered to test vehicles in Spain; the tests are only carried out at special centres. Any faults are noted and you are given time to have them corrected before it is taken back, free of charge, for approval. And, once it is given the all clear, you receive a sticker to display in the windscreen.

By the way, cars used to be given a registration plate that started with a letter or two that identified where they came from. For example, a vehicle bearing a plate that said M 1234 BC would have begun life in Madrid while one with CA as its prefix would have come from Cadiz, and so on. Many like that are still around. The initial letters tell those who know the code which of the 52 provinces in Spain the vehicle originally came from. The numbers and last two letters give an indication as to how old it is.

However, with the new millennium has come a new way of registering vehicles. Now they all have four numbers followed by three letters that are issued in sequence from a central office. All you know now is that 1234 ABC is older than 7890 CDE.

Driving licences

Technically, your driving licence should be that issued by the country in which you are normally resident. However, the recently-introduced United Kingdom photocard driving licence can now be registered at your local traffic department in Spain. If you simply take it along there and have it stamped there is no problem. But an old, pink or green licence will not do. This must either be exchanged for a photocard model which you must have stamped or you can, of course, become the proud owner of a Spanish driving licence if you wish.

This is achieved by presenting your British one at the local traffic department. The process is cheap and straightforward or a *gestor* will do it for you for a flat fee. Until a few years ago, it was an offence not to have a Spanish licence if you were registered as living in Spain and owned a Spanish car. More than one luckless motorist whose papers were presented at a roadside checkpoint had to fork out an on-the-spot penalty for not having swapped his UK document for the local one. The going rate used to be 50,000 pesetas – then around £250.

However, it is still illegal to possess more than one licence.

In Spain, the maximum age permitted for anyone to be a professional driver is 70. For the ordinary driver, be it of four-wheeled or two-wheeled vehicles, there is no such limit. However, after the age of 45 drivers must have a check-up (or at least obtain a certificate from a doctor to say they have had one) every five years. Once you reach the age of 70 the check-ups are annual and your licence is granted year-on-year.

After the age of 65 it is not possible to obtain a new driving licence unless the applicant has previously held a licence of similar or superior category in the past. Keeping a licence rather than letting it lapse and then thinking you will take one out again if you feel like it is, therefore, a more practical option.

Part of the reason for this insistence on only fit older people being allowed to remain on the road is a study carried out in Europe a few years ago into the incidence of traffic accidents among senior citizens. This revealed that while this section of the population may drive less than others in terms of distance, the risk of accident per kilometre did increase in the over 70s and was even greater among women than men. They found the most frequent causes of incidents involved change of direction, road junctions, poor weather and secondary roads, just as they do at any age, except that with more experienced drivers speed did not get a mention. Deficiencies which contributed to accidents were cited as visual, auditory, motor, cardio-circulatory, neuropsychiatric and psychological.

Seat belts

Another area that can lead to trouble is the use of seat belts. The wearing of them has been compulsory for years, just as it has in the UK, and the use of safety belts in the rear seats has been a legal requirement since 1992 in all cars registered after 15th April of that year. However, there are periodic crackdowns on their use and drivers and passengers who fail to belt up may find themselves having to find €90 apiece for the breach of the law.

The *Guardia Civil* and local police have been collaborating in some areas to discover what percentage of drivers and front seat or back seat passengers use safety belts and to what extent this behaviour differs according to the type of road and the length of the journey. They have stressed that people in the back not wearing a seat belt contribute to serious injury not only to themselves but those in the front should they be catapulted forward in the event of a head-on crash.

The Spanish Traffic Department claims that though 16.7 per cent of drivers suffering accidents and not wearing a seat belt in 2002 were killed, only 2.3 per cent of those wearing one at the time of the crash lost their lives.

Worth noting, too, is that if you carry a front-seat passenger under the age of 11 you may be fined – even though they are wearing a seat belt. All under-11s must travel in the back unless the car has special equipment. One grandfather who had just picked up his offspring from the airport discovered this when handed a stiff on-the-spot fine on the way home. The fact that his grandson was within a month of his eleventh birthday did not save him.

Purges are also carried out now and then on motor cyclists whose machines are making too much noise or who are not wearing crash helmets. The legal requirement to wear a crash helmet when riding on a two-wheeled vehicle is complicated in Spain by their language. One of the few words to start with the Y-sounding double L is *llevar* which means not only to wear but 'to carry, transport or bear' (although it should be remembered that pronunciation does vary from one region to another, just as it does in the UK). So, especially in warm weather, you frequently see scooter or motor bike riders with helmets on their elbows. Those with no thought for safety who want to feel the wind wafting through their curls, carry their helmets rather than wear them and *llevar* appears to free them from prosecution.

Selling a vehicle

It was New Year's Day, and still early in the morning, when Alistair's phone rang. The policeman at the other end sounded far from festive when he said, 'Your car's been in an accident.'

'It hasn't,' Alistair informed him. 'I can see it outside where I left it last night and it's perfectly OK.'

'What's the number?' the officer wanted to know. When he was told, he replied, 'Not that car, the other one.' And he gave Alistair another number. It was of a car he had sold four years before. 'You had better come to the station. You're still the registered owner,' he was told.

It was not until September in the following year – 21 months later – that the matter was finally cleared up.

It turned out that the friend who dealt in cars as well as repairing them, to whom Alistair had sold the vehicle, had not fulfilled his promise to register the change of ownership. He had done the car up and sold it on to an Englishwoman who had made the same promise to him. She had not bothered with the paperwork either, but had simply driven the car for three and a half years before passing it on to a young woman who worked in a bar she went into now and then.

A Spanish cook there had borrowed it to get home, and it was he who had had a minor mishap on New Year's Eve and left it by the roadside. When the police checked the number on their files, the trail led them straight to Alistair.

It transpired that the car was in the pound to which the police had removed it. Alistair was told, that as the legal owner, he could collect it. It was in such a state that he did not want it and none of the others in the chain who had driven it wanted it either, so it was scrapped.

Then the payments began. The annual tax – the *Impuesto sobre vehiculos de tracción mechánica* – had not been paid at the town hall since Alistair had sold it and he was still legally responsible for that. He checked and found that with the compounded 20 per cent fines that had accrued for the previous three years, it was a sizeable amount. The woman whose laziness had caused the problem agreed that it was really down to her and went with him to the local town hall and brought the payments up-to-date.

Now, the only way to stop the tax becoming due each year, was to officially 'write off' the vehicle which was already scrapped. The local traffic department refused to do this until the tax for the New Year was paid as the tax had to have been paid for the year in which the *baja* – as the recognised demise of a vehicle is called – was done.

'There's nothing more to pay,' the town hall staff said, however. They repeated it at three different times during the year, too. The advice from the lawyer, who by now was helping sort out the muddle, was to forget about it as it was the town hall which would want paying anyway. If it said nothing was due, that was fine.

However, when car taxes were due the following year, a demand for payment for the old car arrived but only for the current year, not the previous one for which they still insisted nothing was due. Alistair paid it, saw his solicitor and got a *baja* put on the car, at last. The Englishwoman accepted that she was liable for this tax, too, and also paid the solicitor's fee. Phew!

Three months later a demand appeared for the tax Alistair had tried unsuccessfully to pay for the previous year – plus a further 20 per cent fine. That was duly paid, under protest, and – hopefully – that is the end. At least, he has lots of papers to show should the matter be resurrected.

This is not an isolated instance.

The tax delay

A car was sold to a Belgian who agreed to perform the paper trans-actions as part of the price … then went back to Belgium. The tax was relatively small – worth around £30 – and so the town hall did not bother until five or six years had gone by. Then, with the fines, it was worth chasing ... and they did. In this particular case, with the new owner untraceable and the car probably in a Liege junkyard, all the vendor could do was pay the town hall their dues and try and get his name off the register.

As the current owner was not available to sign the required transfer of ownership forms, the only way this predicament could be resolved was for the car to be officially 'exported' at a cost of around £5 (the cost of the export form).

Why don't town halls notify the non-payment of the tax the first year, you may ask? The answer is that it pays to let the money mount. If they inform the legal owners of vehicles whose bills have not been paid immediately, they don't pull in as much money. And allied to that is the fact that legal action can only be taken to recover debts over the equivalent of about £125.

The time it takes to transfer ownership of a vehicle can vary too. One provincial traffic department informed all local *gestors* one June that no changes would be made before September. The reason given was that holidays and staff shortages meant they could only cope with the 700 new vehicles a month being registered in the province. The second-hand backlog had to wait.

As there is a difference in tax structures between mainland Spain and the Canaries, duty may be incurred if a vehicle is brought in from the islands. One owner fell foul of this law for, although he applied for the transfer to mainland plates as soon as the vehicle arrived, he and his wife had bought a house several months before. This made him a legal resident, and it was ruled by the customs authority that the relevant period for the car's registration dated from his arrival and not that of the vehicle. That cost him a couple of thousand pounds.

The preceding tales are random examples purely to illustrate what problems motor vehicles can lead to. Despite the obstacles, many expatriates decide to drive down in their car with United Kingdom plates. It is only then that some find they cannot officially keep them for long ... legally.

A blind eye?

However, all the rules and regulations relating to motor vehicles are so involved that most police forces just don't want to get involved with it all and tend to turn a blind eye on the whole business just as long as you behave yourself. But this does not mean that you will not run into all sorts of difficulties, for instance, if you are involved in an accident, warrant a speeding ticket or prove to be over the drink-drive limit when called on to blow in the machine.

It is not likely that you will run up against officialdom any more often in Spain than you have done before, but the rules are different and it is as well to have at least an outline of them lest you should be called on to play the game.

As for actually being on the road, many people are put off by the hustle and bustle of Spanish driving with its apparently carefree regard for traffic signals and lane markings and with everything on the wrong side of the road. Remember, though, that traffic every-where looks worse from the pavement than it does when you are actually in it and behind the wheel yourself.

Despite the fact that it is as difficult to find a parking space in towns and cities throughout Spain as it is anywhere else, there are many miles of beautifully-crafted motorways where it is still possible to experience the joys of the open road.

10 The quality of life

Why is it better in Spain?

One of the reasons often quoted for making the transition by those who are moving to live in Spain is the better quality of life. Everyone nods and seems to understand what is meant although it is difficult to define. Pace certainly has something to do with it, for once the decision is taken and the centre of a person's universe has shifted to Spain, it is much easier to find time to stop being 'full of care' and just 'stand and stare' or, better yet, sit and stare. The climate takes a hand in this, of course, for it is just not possible to keep rushing around when the thermometer tells you it is pushing 30° out there.

That is where new friendships come in. If people are not moving past one another at such speed, they have more time to talk and this inter-relationship plays a large part in the upturn in what folk get out of life. Time to meet for a coffee; the chance to enjoy a game of golf or bowls; knowing that, in some areas, you can plan a trip into the country or to the beach without the thought of rain intervening; being able to sit outside over dinner until all hours without the need of woollies. These simple pleasures are part of the jigsaw that makes up this picture of a more contented existence.

Then there is the fact that, although prices have surged ahead in Spain as everywhere else in recent years, money still goes further there. And while the euro serves its apprenticeship as a currency, the UK pensioner benefits from an exchange rate that may enable every pound go that much further. Add to that an enormous reduction in heating bills and you have a recipe for improving finances.

By the very nature of things, newcomers find themselves spending more time out of doors, and this is another reason for friendships forming. It is, however, as much a matter of personality in Spain as it is anywhere else. If you have lots of friends in England or Ireland you will soon make new ones in Spain too. If you want to be solitary, it is as easy to avoid expatriates and Spaniards as anybody else.

Mobile phone charges

As for old friends, keeping in touch is not difficult these days with phones and email making letter-writing less essential than in former times. Telephone charges were looked at in Chapter 6, but it is perhaps worth pointing out that the European Commission itself is gearing itself up to take action against mobile phone companies that stand accused of operating in collusion to overcharge customers who use their phones abroad. This applies to Spanish telephones being used in other countries just as much as when British mobiles are taken on to the Continent. Similar investigations into mobile phone companies charging clients when they call someone on another system have taken place within the UK as well. The companies deny price-fixing but the alleged infringements arise from an agreement between them which makes so-called roaming customers pay for incoming as well as outgoing calls.

Language

Keeping in touch by modern methods with former friends is one thing; communicating with neighbours who do not speak your language is another. The need to learn Spanish was looked at in the first chapter and it bears repeating that the ability to understand the idiom of the country in which you are living does help. Just how essential it is depends on where your retirement home is located. Most Brits do tend to congregate in areas where there are lots of other English speakers, and it is obvious that the less anyone intends to integrate into Spanish society the less vital learning the language becomes. However, there is no doubt that anyone living in Spain does benefit from even a basic grasp of the local tongue. Usually it does not take long for all that is necessary for day-to-day pleasantries and getting the shopping done to happen. Beyond that, it is up to the individual, with the need being greater the further from British-dominated communities you choose to live.

This question of location affects other facets of life, too, for in the more popular expatriate retirement areas all sorts of amenities abound. English libraries are on hand as are all kinds of clubs and associations, from Royal British Legion branches to theatre groups, from dance classes to gardening clubs. Many town halls run Spanish classes, which are such a good place to not only learn the language but meet similarly challenged classmates, that they are often over-subscribed with waiting lists. Courses exist in other subjects as well with many foreigners knowledgeable in a variety of subjects from cookery to painting in charge of classes as well as local teachers. U3A (University of the Third Age) courses are available in some areas, and if the expatriate has the ability and the inclination there is encouragement for them to initiate a course in any subject in which they have an enthusiastic interest.

One subject that is much to the fore in many retirement areas is music. Choirs and music societies are unlikely to be missing from the list of local activities and inquiries at the local *Casa de la Cultura* – which as its name implies is the centre of cultural activities in the municipality – will normally prove fruitful. Dance groups and even orchestras are not uncommon, while jazz appreciation brings many into contact with talented instrumentalists who perform in bars and clubs throughout Spain in a truly international mix. Why, the latest national guitar competition was won by a Norwegian.

Churches

Church services of many denominations and in several languages take place in tourist areas alongside the Spanish Roman Catholic ones. There are Catholic priests conducting services in English while the Church of England has clergymen fulfilling parochial duties as well as taking Holy Communion in local churches, hotels and apartment block assembly rooms. Evangelical churches conduct services wherever a few English-speaking residents gather together, and the Baptist and Methodist Churches have congregations on the *costas*. How important the church is in the lives of many people was evident a few years ago when the BBC brought its popular 'Songs of Praise' programme to southern Spain and ended with two thousand singers serenading bathers on the beach at Torremolinos.

Muslim mosques and Jewish synagogues co-exist with the Kingdom Halls of Jehovah's Witnesses, and Presbyterian Scots may find their place of worship referred to in the list of services in the local newspaper next to those of the Church of Jesus Christ of Latter Day Saints, the Dutch Evangelical Church, a Baha'i meeting, the First Church of Christ, Scientist, or the Scandinavian ministry. Church attendance may be falling in the UK but it is clear that religious observance in its many forms is alive and well among the expatriates of Iberia.

The media

Having mentioned the press it is well to draw attention to the proliferation of what might be termed 'the media' aimed at English-speaking Spanish residents.

Newspapers

English national papers are available in Spain each morning with most of them having been printed in Spain. If you are not in a tourist area, they will probably not be in the local newsagent's, but in the main retirement areas expatriates can keep in touch with their favourite columnists and cartoons as well as abreast of the particular slant on the news they are used to. They will not cost 30p or 40p though, for the Spanish editions run from €1.70 or €1.80 for tabloids to €2.50 for *The Daily Telegraph*, with the Sundays commensurately expensive and costing from €2.70 upwards.

There are local newspapers of varying quality in every area where advertising will sustain them and many are free. This is down to the fact that the first ones were given away and this has proved a cycle difficult to break. There are signs, though, that some people are prepared to pay a modest cover price if it means a better-quality product. Many magazines also focus on the expatriate market with a few long-term survivors and a more or less constant stream of others coming and going. The problem for any new publication is that there are just too many of them after the same advertisers along with the radio and television stations that prolif-erate – Spanish as well as foreign. Unless a niche can be found or a wider pool of advertising clients attracted, the life of any new attempt to inform or entertain the public depends on the depth of the pocket of the backer.

Radio

The British resident will probably be surprised at the choice of English-language radio stations. At one point the number attempting to cater for their listening for at least part of the day reached double figures on the Costa del Sol alone. If the choice is for a spot of local Spanish radio – to help with the language, for instance – the selec-tion is bewildering everywhere. At the moment in Málaga province alone there are 19 local radio stations adding to the national ones. Worth noting is that among the national ones is Spain's classic music channel on 98.1 FM. This will appeal to anyone who likes lis-tening to the world's greatest composers and performers. It has been described by a musician who played in one of Britain's major orchestras all around the world before retiring to Spain as the best classical music channel he has ever discovered.

Local TV

Which local television station to watch is less of a problem for the Brit as Spanish-based English TV consists of odd programmes for them interspersed among local Spanish programmes. And 'odd' can be the appropriate word, too. However, if you want to see what the locals are watching, you will have several stations to check out (11 on the Costa del Sol alone). Nationwide, there are half a dozen major channels with the sort of soaps, discussions and celebrity event mix-ture that viewers will be used to. The Spanish love of sport is reflected with coverage of many minor as well as major events, and the value of prizes on the quiz shows (like an apartment or two cars) can be much greater than you are used to back home. And watching them can help you become more familiar with the language.

Transport

A detailed look at things affecting the motorist occupied the preceding chapter, but what about public transport? After all, being able to get around does have a marked effect on how pleasant life is going to be. Local buses are like local buses everywhere – they vary not only from district to district but from route to route. Generally though, the matter of getting from place to place in the tourist areas is no great hardship, always with the proviso that traffic conditions may affect bus times so that the old adage about none coming and then three being there all at once applies.

Fares are cheaper than those in the UK and a huge difference is noticeable on the railways in this regard. Local rail services are used with satisfaction by many Brits where they provide connecting links to mainline terminals. With the distances involved in getting from city to city in Spain that much greater, rail links are important and the network of high-speed trains running between major centres is being extended. Many normally car-bound Brits who spend holidays in Spain find getting around on public transport is sufficiently good for them to feel no need to drive and, by choosing the right location to live, some permanent residents do without their own car as well.

Pensioners may be able to obtain concessionary cards from their local rail and bus stations, on proof of age and residence. Renfe, the state rail company, can be asked anywhere, but local bus discounts depend on where you are. It will cost nothing to find out, though the savings on local bus routes may prove minimal.

Taxi services are always available in the tourist spots and, while having a vehicle of your own is handy, it is worthwhile checking out whether simply calling for a taxi when one is needed might not work out less expensive when compared with a car's high insurance costs as well as fuel and repair bills. Do not forget to ask a taxi driver what the fare will be before you get in. All charges are regulated, but the unsuspecting are sometimes more than literally taken for a ride.

Another factor to be borne in mind in this context is that car hire is much cheaper in Spain. Indeed, if a car is only being used for shopping and infrequent local trips, public transport with taxis as part of the deal and a day's car hire for off-route trips now and then, may work out more economical than having a few thousand pounds tied up in something which is not strictly necessary.

Alcohol

The quality of life of many expatriates living in Spain is affected by alcohol and the places providing it. Bars can be places to meet people, sources of entertainment and the venue for indoor sporting activities. For many they become the centre for their socialising. But, with the far cheaper cost of beverages than in the UK, they can easily become the entire focus of life for some who retire to the sun. Anyone who has joined an expatriate community will be able to cite instances where acquaintances became so caught up in this bar culture that the only question was whether their money or their liver gave out first.

A Canadian who has lived in various parts of the world and runs a Spanish branch of the Lions' Club makes a point of telling all new residents he comes across: 'Here's the best advice anyone will give you. Keep out of the bars! It's just too easy to spend the rest of your life sitting in the same place with a glass in your hand.' His warning is passed on for consideration.

However, everywhere there are branches of Alcoholics Anonymous so there must be something in what he says. Local newspapers carry advertisements with helpful telephone numbers for English speakers, and all clinics have details of free phone lines to ring if you are one of those who needs help in giving up either of the two popular drugs – alcohol and tobacco. The local population clearly includes those who find such assistance helps, too.

Grandmother's teaching about the Devil finding work for idle hands still applies. The beauty of retiring to Spain is that there are so many things to do that nobody has any cause to be idle … unless they simply feel like being lazy.

11 Pets and pastimes

Taking pets to Spain

Some people feel their pets will prevent them from moving out of the United Kingdom. 'If we go and live in Spain what will happen to them?' they fret. The answer is, 'Take them with you.'

There is no problem about taking your animal companion along on the adventure. As long as they are in good health there is no obstacle to their emigrating too. But requirements have changed in recent years and, with the expanding and ever-changing needs of the new Europe, they will almost certainly continue to change.

For instance, the British foot-and-mouth outbreak of 2001, hot on the heels of the BSE scare, made a frightened Continent look more closely at any animal crossing the Channel – whether alive and kicking or as meat from an abattoir. However, it is still relatively easy to take a dog or cat to Spain. Animals must be accompanied by their owners who have a certificate, including a Spanish translation, saying they have been under the owner's supervision for three months before importation, that they are not intended for trade and that the owners accept allowing medical checks by recognised vets. Except for those under three months old, they will also need a certificate of origin and health that is valid for just 10 days and shows they have had anti-rabies inoculation. It is bringing them back into the UK that is complicated and expensive.

The PETS scheme for re-entry

For up-to-date information on what is necessary, you can ring the helpline set up by the UK Government under the Pet Travel Scheme operated by DEFRA (the Department for Environment, Food and Rural Affairs). This PETS Helpline is available from

8.30am to 5pm Monday to Friday by phone on 0870 241 1710 or by fax on 020 7904 6834. From outside the UK, dial 00 for the international switchboard, 44 for the UK and then omit the first 0 of the number. You can also contact PETS by email on pets.helpline@defra.gsi.gov.uk or on their website which is www.defra.gov.uk/animalh/quarantine.

To qualify for the PETS scheme your pet must be fitted with a microchip and vaccinated against rabies, but not before it is three months old. It must also be blood-tested at a laboratory recognised by DEFRA to show that the vaccination was effective, but your pet may not enter the UK until six months have passed from the date that your vet took the successful blood sample. If a vet signs the pet's export certificate after that six month period has elapsed, the pet may then enter the UK immediately.

Your pet must also be issued with an official PETS certificate (PETS 1) by a government-authorised veterinarian to verify that these procedures have been carried out. There must also be an official certificate to show that it has been treated against ticks and tapeworm. This certificate must be in English and the treatment carried out between 24 and 48 hours before it is checked in for the return journey. Pets travelling on a sea crossing or by rail must accompany passengers with a vehicle which can make this compliance difficult. There is no problem if you are heading south, but if you intend to take a pet back into the UK a call to the PETS Helpline could avoid a hold up at the special PETS entry point at the docks.

Then you need a signed declaration (PETS 3) to say your pet has not been outside the PETS country during the six months before travelling to the UK, something which should be done on the day you travel back to the UK though obviously you will need to have the form in advance via the PETS Helpline or from your transport company.

Air travel for pets

If you are travelling by air in either direction your pet must be in an airline approved travel carrier and this container must be large enough to allow the animal to move without restriction. All animals travelling under PETS have to be sent to the UK as cargo, not as excess baggage, and passengers must be booked separately. The only exceptions are for guide and hearing dogs on some routes where they may travel in the cabin.

The cost for all this is not cheap and the pet's airfare will be more than that for the owner. At the beginning of 2003 the single airway bill for a dog heading for Heathrow or Gatwick from Málaga, Sevilla, Alicante or Valencia was €592.60. A second dog on the same ticket cost €278.87. A cat's fare was €536.82 with a second travelling for €244.01. From Palma de Mallorca the dog fare was €509.24 (€258.68 for a second) and €468.64 for a cat (the second went for €225.04). These prices all included 16 per cent IVA (the equivalent of British VAT) and were those charged by a company based near Málaga. They included reception charges in Spain, carriage to London, custom clearance and animal reception centre charges on arrival. They point out that freight charges may vary at any time.

For years, there was a six-month quarantine period in Ministry-approved kennels to be paid for, and this can still apply from some destinations, though not Spain unless the demands of the PETS scheme are not met The main reason touted for this to be neces-sary was rabies, which those in the know found ridiculous. A Spanish vet explained to one lady wanting to take her pet back to England with her, 'I've been a vet for more than 10 years, and when I was doing my training at college all of us wanted to see an animal with rabies so that we would know first hand what we were dealing with. It proved impossible as there wasn't a case in Spain we could go and see. We all agreed that if we heard of a case we would tell each other immediately so we could see a stricken animal some time in the future.

'Since then I still haven't seen one. There has been one case up near the Pyrenees, but it was an isolated animal and by the time I heard about it the chance had gone. To all intents and purposes there is no rabies in Iberia and all the fuss your people make looks like it is just to make money for people with kennels.'

The requirement that a microchip be inserted into your pet applies in several places within Spain now, too. The process is painless and once the tiny electronic bug is under their skin, any policeman with a scanning device can tell whose dog it is. The plan safeguards valuable and cherished dogs from theft and has helped reduce the number of strays, for any dogs unaccompanied on the street and taken to the pound can be identified. The owner is then notified and unless they turn up within the specified time and pay the fine for allowing their pet to stray, the dog is lost forever. Dogs not electronically recognisable are either found a home through a pet rescue service or put down.

Outdoor sports and pursuits

For those interested in sport, Spain offers a fantastic range of facilities with the blessing of a climate that encourages outdoor activity. Those with an interest in football will know that *La Liga* is contested by some of the best clubs in the world with the top Spanish and English Premiership sides currently challenging for domination of the European scene. Soccer is an obsession with the Spanish and the Mediterranean region boasts such entertaining sides as Barcelona, Valencia and Málaga in the top flight while there are lesser leagues hosting clubs representing every town and village in the land. Several times a season the giants of Real Madrid and Barcelona meet in combat, and it is then that the whole country splits into one or other camp in much the same way that Glasgow is divided into blue and green halves when Rangers and Celtic clash. Forget the bullfight. This is where Spanish passion is really in evidence.

Golf

Of course, the sport which has made Spain the Mecca for thousands of European players is golf. So many courses offer a first-rate challenge to the golfer along the southern coastline that road signs officially declare 'Costa del Sol/Costa del Golf' lest there should be any doubt about where you are. It is relatively recently that the

Spanish have taken to the sport themselves and courses have sprung up, and are still springing up, all over the country. The appearance of names like Ballesteros, Olazábal, Jiménez and García among Ryder Cup players has done much to foster this growth.

Unlike in the UK, however, where many are municipally owned, most layouts in Iberia are privately controlled and funded. This is due largely to the fact that golf courses are not regarded entirely as open land but are *urbanisable* – that is, land on which building can take place. Most courses encompass private homes, from millionaire's villas to more modest townhouses or apartment blocks, and hotels. In some cases the fairways are like green streets running through the painted properties.

Homes alongside the courses tend to be relatively more expensive than similar property in the area. This is not only because there are those who feel it worthwhile to pay for immediate access from the back garden to the fairway, but because of the safeguard being on a golf course provides. Lots of owners of such villas and townhouses do not play the game, the draw for them being the knowledge that they have well-maintained parkland to look out over and that their view is guaranteed, for nobody is going to be given permission to build a further development on the green their balcony overlooks.

Some homes also offer the inducement that, along with the deeds, comes membership of the club. Indeed, there are some highly-priced properties, the ownership of which is the only means of access to some of the more exclusive courses.

Fees can be high, with £100 being necessary to secure a day on some courses while other still excellent sunshine golf costs nearer £20 a round.

Bowls

Another British import which has spread on the expatriate-populated coasts and islands is lawn bowls. Perhaps it was the association with Sir Francis Drake that stemmed much initial interest among the locals – or maybe it was their involvement with *petanca*, the game which can be played anywhere, and which is called *boules* by the French. Steadily, the sport-loving Spaniards are joining their new neighbours to play the game, however, and fine lawn or artificial rinks are available to those who fancy a game pretty well everywhere. Indeed there are leagues which see competing teams visit one another's greens in stiff competition, the season being during the winter … it's just too hot in the middle of the year and many players head north at that time in any case.

Other ball games

Cricket is another imported sport enjoyed in Spain, again with league games played during the winter when conditions in many parts of the country are much like the English summer – including the rainy days that stop play. However, the players are almost exclusively from Britain or the Commonwealth with the locals mystified by the proceedings. Spectators, scorers and umpires are welcomed as well as those who still fancy a game. Tennis is available everywhere with councils providing courts as well as others being available at hotels or as part of communities.

Whether it is golf, bowls, cricket, tennis or *petanca* you fancy, it is simply a matter of asking around in the area you are looking to live in, whether on the islands or on the mainland, if you intend keeping an interest in your particular sport alive.

Horse riding

Horses are probably more in evidence throughout Spain than they are in the UK, particularly in the South and in Extremadura, as well as on farms all over the country. Riding schools and mounts for hire are easy to come by. Many Spaniards keep their own horses which come out on parade during high days and holidays, and you will be unlucky if there is not a stable near you where you can maintain contact with horses if you wish. Pony trekking is part of the holiday facilities on offer in several places and there is wonderful countryside to view from horseback.

Water sports

Water sports are naturally very much in evidence along the coast. As well as municipal swimming pools, many homes and communities have their own and, of course, swimmers make the most of beach facilities throughout much of the year in the south of the country. Harbours continue to be built and extended all along the coasts and they are increasing the facilities for every type of activity in, on or under the water. Whether it is sailing or scuba diving which attracts, there are sure to be facilities for learning or continuing a hobby not far from any home on the coast.

Angling

Angling is another popular pastime that does not have to be left behind in a move to Spain. All types of sea angling are available, from shark fishing trips on the Mediterranean to rock fishing or taking on the challenge of the surf beaches on the Atlantic seaboard. A pole, a spool of line and a few hooks and floats are all that are required to give hours of pleasure among the locals from harbour walls or rocky outcrops all along the shore. Spanish saltwater anglers use much longer rods than are to be seen on UK beaches, many of them of the telescopic type at which British surfcasters would turn up their noses. They do keep line clear of the surf and swell, though. Reels are large fixed-spool models with multipliers only used for boat expeditions.

Despite the dry climate, inland there is much sport that is virtually untapped. With the proliferation of reservoirs during Franco's time, many streams have been dammed and the new lakes created stocked with fish. Native barbel soon established themselves in many of them with imported bass finding the warm water to their liking. There are pike, too, along with goldfish that have acclimatised after release from bowls they outgrew as unwanted fairground prizes. In streams in the north and in the Pyrenees there are trout that will take a fly, and there are even one or two game fishing spots in the south.

But the quarry most sought by the British angler in Spanish fresh-water is the carp. It takes a lot of time or luck to discover the best areas in waters that are enormous by British standards. And there are many private banks as well as inaccessible cliffs that restrict just where angling is possible. Asking around will normally reveal popular places, however, and the angler is much more likely to find elusive 20, or even 30, pounders in Iberia than in the UK, even in the Canaries. The sort of tackle British carp specialists would want to use is not always available and bait can also be difficult to find – or expensive. So take your gear with you. Nobody who enjoys the Gentle Art need leave their tackle behind when they retire to Spain.

One very important word of warning is necessary, however. Make sure you have a licence with you when you go fishing! The bailiff who asked for your permit in England was not armed with a machine-gun. It is likely that the one who approaches you in Spain will be, for it is the *Guardia Civil* that is charged with patrolling the banks and protecting the environment, especially in nature reserves where much of the good fishing is to be found. *Guardia Civil* officers have the right to confiscate tackle from anyone fishing without authorisation … and they exercise it.

Take your English licence to Spain with you. To obtain a licence in Andalucía, for instance, applicants must prove their competence by producing a local licence for any two of the previous five years – or the would-be angler has to sit a multiple-choice examination … in Spanish of course. However, a licence to fish from another part of Spain or another country is accepted as proof that they know how to behave on the bank. So bring the one from the Environment Agency with you so that you can avoid unnecessary hassle.

In some parts of Spain you can simply buy a licence but be sure it is for the water you intend to fish. For instance, Michael – an Englishman who has lived in Spain for years and understands the rules – made a point of obtaining a licence when he went on holiday to fish for catfish in the River Ebro where Germans in particular camp out every summer to take specimens that weigh more than they do themselves. The first day, a Friday, he was accosted by armed guards who informed him that he was on the wrong bank. His licence was for Cataluña but he was on the Aragón side of the river for which his permit was not valid. They took his rods, and before he could get them back he would have to make a special trip to Zaragoza to obtain the correct licence. There he found the office would not be open again until the Monday. It was only by showing the correct piece of paper back at the local police headquarters that he got his rods back so that he could start fishing again – a round trip of around 300 kilometres and a waste of three days.

If in doubt, the place to inquire about a licence is a tackle shop. You will probably be directed to the local council's environment office (called *Medio Ambiente*) or a local bank or government building. They are cheap enough, just a nuisance to get. One great feature though is that once you turn 65 you will never need another one for, once you are a pensioner, your angling licence lasts forever, at least in Andalucía.

Shooting

Shooting is also available and popular, with Spain's red-leg partridges famous throughout the world of country sportsmen. As with deer and wild boar – both of which are also found on large, private reserves as well as the protected natural parks – to pursue these quarry it is best to make an approach to one of those advertising such amenities. They can advise on gun laws as well as appropriate weapons and ammunition, for what firearms can be taken and used where can be confusing within the changing legislation of the countries comprising the European Union. Unless your Spanish is fluent, it is also wise to ensure you are not the only English speaker on a shoot, and consequently not totally aware of local custom, by first looking for access via an English shooting periodical rather than one of the Spanish ones.

Many of the restrictions covering country sport have been formulated with shooting in mind as pursuit of game with a gun is more popular in Spain than angling. As a result things taken for granted by

British fishermen – like groundbaiting and the use of catapults – can land the innocent in an embarrassing situation in some places. If it were thought they were putting bait down to attract deer or boar, for example, the sportsman might have to answer some awkward questions. Ask around and be sure before you find yourself in trouble. Night fishing is universally prohibited throughout Spain though there are places where a blind eye is turned. However, it pays not to take chances.

Like shooters, anglers will find trips to prolific waters organised by genuine guides. But beware of some of the local entrepreneurial types who crop up from time to time and tell novice fishermen, for instance, that they can take them to special waters where no licence is needed. They charge an extortionate amount for taking the unwary to places where they could go for nothing themselves but with the risk that they could get all their gear impounded.

Rambling

Ramblers will find Spain to their liking, for there are vast tracts of land with marked paths that will take them into wild country where eagles will be overhead, and there is the chance of seeing deer or wild boar. Groups often get together to share these walks and local newspapers or libraries will know who to contact. Several have found that it only takes a few neighbours to share a car for a rambling group to spring up. The benefit is that all of them soon begin to get to new places that one or other of them has discovered.

Organised holidays are available as well, with walkers wending their way through unspoilt countryside while their luggage is transported from inn to hotel or *hostal* ahead of them. They are more expensive than wandering into the mountains on your own but do ensure accommodation at reasonable interludes – and lighten the load.

Bird watching

Bird watching, too, will delight in Spain. Those who have enjoyed the hobby before find there is the chance to observe species they had not seen in Britain, while people who have never been interested become curious to find out more about the colourful visitors to their garden or terrace.

Being on a main migratory route, Iberia is the place to see a huge variety of birds. Familiar friends like swallows, swifts and martins that have been heard screeching during summer evenings all over the Continent pass through in the autumn in company with a multitude of starlings. Flocks of buzzards and osprey that have nested in Scandinavia or Scotland wheel southward on the air, while visitors such as vultures that come to Spain for the warm months cross back over the Straits of Gibraltar with them.

Bee eaters that cause a stir when they are spotted infrequently performing their aerial acrobatics in Britain, and the colourful hoopoe, are sighted so often in southern Spain that nobody bothers to comment on the fact, and egrets ride on the backs of sheep and goats just as they make use of wild life on the African veldt. Birds head down the length of the Portuguese coast or from France round the eastern end of the Pyrenees to follow the Mediterranean shore south. Others navigate their way across Spain from the Bay of Biscay and follow valleys that rivers have carved through the coastal mountains to join them.

A party set out one autumn day to watch passing birds of prey near Tarifa, that town on a promontory whose corsairs intercepting merchant vessels heading through the Straits of Gibraltar gave the word 'tariff' to the English language. In the single day they logged 11 different raptor species.

Another bird watcher used powerful binoculars to read the number on a ring on the leg of a common gull he spotted on a Mediterranean beach in winter and found it had been tagged on the Bristol Channel the summer before. Exactly a year later, he identified the same bird again and then discovered that it had been listed back in south Wales in the meantime. And to think that humans who need a car, train or even an airplane to make the same journey call such a creature 'common'.

Unfortunately, nightingales that were heard year after year in the Balearics and many other places have all but disappeared due to the enormous amount of construction during the last 20–30 years.

Biking

The scope for increased enjoyment also applies to those who fancy mountain biking. Cycles are for hire in some places and there are many kilometres of track that wind through valleys and around mountains. Sometimes, holiday groups are led on organised expeditions. If anyone fancies it, the answer, again, is just to ask around. The same goes for cycling proper, for there is great interest in professional cycle racing with *La Vuelta*, Spain's version of the Tour de France, hitting the headlines while every region stages its own championships.

For those who don't want to be that energetic, motor scooters are for hire, and most tourist areas have jeep safaris going off into untamed wilderness not far away. Almost any outdoor activity is available if you just look for it.

Many people who are thinking of retiring will not be too interested in the athletics tracks or basketball courts provided in most towns but, as a result of the interest in gymnastics in Spain, facilities are available for those who want to keep up a fitness routine. Private as well as council-run gymnasiums abound and most have skilled staff who will work out a programme for anyone, regardless of age, weight and physical ability. Increasingly, they have a sauna available, too, which some find more agreeable.

Gardening

One outdoor pastime that provides great pleasure for numerous people in Spain is gardening. Plants that are blighted by the frost will thrive all year round in many parts of Spain and the timing on seed packets can be ignored. Plants such as runner beans, which in England must be sown in April or May can be put in at Christmas. Hibiscus, petunias and the Busy Lizzy can provide colour in the middle of winter. In fact, the gardening year is more or less reversed in the South of Spain, for plants need a rest at some stage and here it is during the heat of the summer. Burned and dry, they tend to die back then rather than when expected by the British whose gardens are frozen or disappear under snow for their 'down' season.

A huge disappointment in the past decade has been the demise of the geranium. It was common to see a dozen different varieties in all sorts of colours of bloom and leaf in a garden but that awful pest, the geranium bronze butterfly, arrived from South Africa and decimated all but a few. This thumb-nail-sized insect lays eggs which turn into maggots that burrow straight into the soft centre of the stalk. The first the gardener knows is when his geraniums wilt and collapse, for the maggot eats away the core of the plant with only a shrivelled outer layer left around a black centre. Spraying every fortnight can keep the pest away, but many have taken to growing other plants instead.

Local nurseries, called *viveros*, are everywhere and, along with stalls on all markets that sell plants just as cheaply, terraces and gardens can be kept in bloom throughout the 12 months. It is fun for the northern European to harvest fruit, vegetables and flowers out of season. Indeed, it is possible to have three crops of potatoes, for example, from the same plot in the same year though, obviously, not on a regular basis. One country town, famous for its potatoes, exports its entire crop to the UK.

And, of course, the sight of bougainvillea and the scent of jasmine are integral parts of the image of Spain. How nice to have them outside your own door, either in a garden or in pots on the terrace.

Indoor pursuits

Indoors, all kinds of sport are available everywhere with pool and darts leagues flourishing. Snooker halls can be found and a game called *Billard*, which is played on a half-size snooker table with no pockets (that's right, no pockets and you just play cannons) is fairly universal. For anyone fancying their chess prowess, Spain is surprisingly blessed with clubs everywhere and lots of open tournaments offering tempting prizes if you think you are good enough. It is a good way to meet Spaniards of all ages and, of course, language is no barrier here. But, unless you are more than adequately competent, don't expect to win too often.

Dancing

Maybe not a sport, but certainly energetic, is line dancing. The craze has taken a firm hold in Spain, and groups of dancers wearing Stetsons and high-heeled boots meet regularly to be put through their paces. Then they put on displays at all sorts of venues and events. The way in which it keeps women of a certain age fit and then provides entertainment has almost made it rival flamenco in some places.

And, of course, flamenco itself, along with music and dance from other local traditions, must not be overlooked. Foreigners who become interested in these traditional dance routines are welcome and many do join in classes. Indeed, some classes are even run by non-Spanish instructors who have become immersed in the local culture.

Computers

Computers, the Internet and the world wide web have become such an integral part of many lives these days that it may be stretching a point to consider them as a pastime. However, if they are not being used in a commercial capacity but for Free Cell games, creating images with Picture Publisher and keeping check on finances with Quicken, they are not so much a tool for work as a form of leisure pursuit.

Anything anyone may want to do with computers can be accomplished as easily in Spain as anywhere else. Whatever new equipment is required is available and at prices not dissimilar from those in the UK. One thing to watch, unless you have really got to grips with the language, is that you do not wind up with the latest programme that is all the more difficult to understand because the 'Help' is in Spanish. Battling with Spanish instructions might be a good way of improving your language skills, but – if you are not prepared for it – the added difficulty could prove a way of ensuring the computer is dumped and never used again. This is a possibility to bear in mind.

As in most countries, there are Internet cafés where you can go online for a hired period, and facilities exist in some places for library users to have on hand modern electronic methods of research and reference.

Hopefully with more time to read than during a busy career, many pensioners make the most of libraries. In tourist areas in Spain there are often English sections in public libraries where staff – sometimes British volunteers – tend to the needs of borrowers. There is also a thriving market in second-hand books at places like boot sales where a few *centimos* (100 of which make up the Spanish euro) can provide hours of enjoyment.

Volunteers and enthusiasts

On the subject of volunteers, it is worth noting that those who master Spanish are always in demand to assist as interpreters at health clinics or police stations, while anyone – bilingual or not – who wants to expand their contacts will find a welcome at charity shops or the local library.

Painting, sculpture and pottery are activities often taken up by those with time on their hands to follow their inclinations. Art classes are a popular part of programmes encouraged by most local authorities, along with most of the other courses on offer at evening classes in the UK. It is fair to say that if you have a sphere of interest, there is a way of pursuing it once you move to Spain.

12 Health care

The Spanish health system

One thing that motor vehicles and human beings have in common is that as they become older the need for repairs and maintenance increases. For the peace of mind of all concerned it is good to know that should something go wrong there is a competent garage on hand in the one case and a functioning clinic available in the other … and that you can afford them.

As far as health care is concerned, it is generally agreed that the Spanish state system functions more efficiently than the one you have been used to in the UK. That is not to say that it is better in all respects, but when you do need treatment it is usually available more readily. The odds are that if you need a serious operation (and aren't they all serious for those concerned) it will be performed rather more quickly. Many doctors and nurses speak at least some English, and in areas where significant numbers of tourists make use of the local medical facilities interpreters are on hand. Bands of volunteers man desks at clinics and often provide transport and moral support for hospital visits as well.

Different nursing

However, one thing that does come as something of a shock to British patients in Spain is that nurses do just that – nurse! They are not expected to provide assistance with serving food or dealing with bedpans as is still expected of British nursing and care staff. Ancillary staff do offer some assistance, but it is anticipated that family members will supply much of the input in what might be termed welfare areas. In private hospitals, full cover may be available but medical insurance does not normally stretch to pay for this and there may be a bill for support which would be considered part of the medical care in the UK.

The plus side of this is that the only-two-visitors-to-a-bed rule is unheard of (except in intensive care units), and the whole family often turn up and lend a hand, with friends and neighbours taking part in after-care as well. It is common for a wife to sleep in a comfortable chair by her husband's hospital bedside overnight to see to toilet arrangements and the like with medical staff on call only if they are needed for their professional skills. The downside of this is that it can feel like market day in the ward when you are trying to recover from the anaesthetic while a dozen noisy folk appear to be holding a party around the next bed.

The follow-up care may vary widely, and across the boundaries of state and private facilities, too. Some may be left to hop out of hospital to find a taxi after an operation on their varicose veins with no assistance in sight in the one case, while in an emergency department down the road staff will insist on a patient with a broken wrist being transported around the place in a wheelchair.

So, how do you gain access to the state's health care when in Spain?

Health forms

The most important form for most of those retiring to Spain to obtain before leaving the UK is the form E121 which gives access to the Spanish health system for British State Retirement pensioners, their spouses and dependent children, and for anyone receiving the UK Incapacity Benefit. Armed with this form, you will be treated like a Spaniard. As has been pointed out, the way you are looked after tends to be different from in the UK, but it is effective and generally much quicker as far as serious problems are concerned.

Too many people living in Spain rely on the E111. This is a form for tourists and covers emergencies only – nothing else. If you have a chronic problem or a pre-existing disease, in theory the Spanish can say 'We are not going to treat you because you have not got the E121'. That is, unless and until you pay.

Some areas may limit the duration of E111 which affects its effectiveness, but not all. The way in which it is checked out varies considerably as well, with some districts being strict as to dates and just who is covered while some hospitals barely bother to look at it. This is largely because individual cases are not referred back to the UK any more than treatment for Spaniards in the UK is billed individually to the Spanish government for payment. All the countries which are part of the common health policy within Europe may have different ways of dealing with matters within their own borders, but they all pay a levy into a common pot and it is from this that the cost of treatment is shared out. It is easy to see how Spain, with around 50 million tourists who may need to make use of its medical facilities in any one year, might well have to provide assistance to many more than the number of Spaniards liable to receive medical help abroad under this reciprocal arrangement.

The health form E109 may come into the picture, but it is for those who are self-employed or employed within an EC country. However, you will probably have to pay the social security payments of that country for it to come into effect. It is more likely to be of use to those paying in Spain to gain cover for someone in the UK. But, as far as getting benefits while living abroad is concerned, the form the State pensioner wants is E121. Without it you will be charged.

Details are all in a booklet (*Going Abroad and Social Security Benefits* which is SA 29) which you should be able to find at your local social security office. In case of any difficulty, it is obtainable from The Pension Service, The Department for Work and Pensions, at Newcastle-upon-Tyne. The full address and phone number are given in Chapter 16.

Help in the home

One of the requirements for towns is that they must provide a home-help type service. But anyone wanting such assistance must be registered as a resident to make use of that system. This is only fair. If you need help with a problem in the home – for instance, if you are unfit and cannot look after yourself properly – you can ask the council to provide some sort of assistance in the home. This could be a cleaner or somebody to do some cooking or do shopping or something of that nature. But you must be registered to receive this help.

This registration, or *empadronamiento*, does not involve any fiscal problems. As detailed in Chapter 8 on town halls and taxes, filling in a form at the local town hall is all that is required, and the information is not passed on to tax authorities or anybody else.

There is another health form – Number 106 – which may be useful for some people. This covers those living but not working in Spain and entitles them to health care cover for themselves and any dependent family members under the state scheme, but lasts for a limited time only. How long depends on whether you can still receive short-term Benefit from the UK if you claim it. Once this entitlement ends, the UK will not provide you with any more health cover. So, if you are under pensionable age on your date of departure, it is Form E106 which is the appropriate certificate to request help. Ask the staff at the Pensions Service in Newcastle about form E106 before leaving the UK if E121 for pensioners is not going to provide for your specific needs.

Private cover

Once you are in possession of the appropriate information, you will be able to decide whether you need to pay for private health cover. Several companies offer to provide for your medical requirements, and the degree to which you will want to make use of their services will depend on your state of health and your bank balance. If you are likely to travel around the world, particularly to North America, that may also be a factor in deciding what medical insurance you are likely to need. If you avail yourself of one of their schemes, make sure you understand the small print, as in all insurance matters.

Gerald was one Englishman who paid for what he believed was total cover when he retired to Spain. He informed the insurance company after he had had a heart attack and was receiving excellent treatment at the local hospital to which the ambulance that had been called had taken him. When his condition was stabilised after some time in intensive care and he was about to be discharged, he was presented with a bill for the equivalent of £4,500. But the insurance company would be paying for it, he pointed out. Oh, no, the hospital told him. If he had had an operation they would have paid for it, but no incision and no trip to the theatre had been necessary, so the cover he had paid for did not come into effect, the small print saw to that.

What saved him £4,500 – and possibly a relapse – was form E121. Once he produced that, they were satisfied that all was well and informed him that there had been no need for the private cover at all. The reciprocal agreement between the NHS and the Spanish health service had provided for his treatment which had been exactly the same whether paying privately or not.

An English nurse living in Spain encountered similar problems with the details of her policy. It also covered her son and, as boys will, he had an accident on his cycle ... or rather off it. He hit the curb and stuck a hand through the glass on a notice board as he fell, causing serious bleeding. The local clinic treated him, but when his mother contacted the insurance company they refused to pay out because the policy in question had a clause covering negligence which they claimed had caused the injury and they were bringing it into play.

But having no cover can prove costly. A couple living in Spain with no health protection discovered that the wife needed a hip replacement operation. They were told that the price would be the same in the UK or Spain, so to restore her to full mobility they paid about £6,000 at a private clinic in England.

In another case, Mollie had taken out a modest health policy but had not read the small print. She was in good health and did not antici-pate any problems. When she needed a hip replacement, the operation went well. But a few days later, while she was still in her hospital bed, she was presented with a steep bill for the prosthesis by the supplier with a demand for immediate payment. Fortunately, her cousin who was with her was able to write out a cheque on the spot. But who knows what would have happened if she had not been able to pay at once!

Incidentally, to get a *residencia*, you must show that you have health insurance (see Chapter 2).

Waiting times

Not that in Spain there are no waiting lists. There are, and it depends on what treatment is needed and where you live, in the same way that the system meets specific requirements in the UK.

For instance, it was in March that Joe began to feel the discomfort in his left leg that a doctor had warned him about years before. He saw a doctor at the local clinic and told him that he was afraid that after all this time his varicose veins would need sorting out. A visit to the nearby hospital's cardiology department confirmed this, and he was given a date several months hence for a further examination. Therefore, it was in September that he was officially diagnosed as needing an operation. However, as a second-class patient (he was glad not to be a top priority) he was told to report back in December, as he would be listed on the following year's calendar.

A scheme which has been talked about a good deal in the UK since, was up and running in Spain and he was offered the chance to have his operation at a private clinic. Important operations, like heart valve replacements, were taking up the time of the surgeons at the major hospital but, if he wished, he could be dealt with elsewhere. He did, and was slotted in for a further examination by the surgeon who would perform the deed. As a result, his successful operation took place free of charge at a private hospital in June ... 15 months after his initial approach, of which time he had been on the waiting list for three or six, he was not sure.

Marjorie was in need of an operation on the cataracts which were developing on both eyes. She was told she would have to wait as, until they were sufficiently developed, they could not be operated on. Several months went by before further examinations resulted in the decision that more delay would be advisable. More months, more tests and then she was informed that there was a consider-able backlog. She told the lady eye surgeon that she was so concerned about the danger in crossing roads when she could no longer see what was coming and fed up with not recognising neigh-bours until they spoke to her, that she would pay to have the cataract on the worse eye removed privately. The result was that the same surgeon performed the operation within a fortnight – at a cost of €1,700.

But in Spain, as in the UK, as long as there are people who are will-ing to pay for private medical attention and doctors who can fill the need, there will always be waiting lists. If any state health service were to function in an ideal manner, with those suffering the most being dealt with promptly and everyone catered for within a rea-sonable period, the need for private care would disappear.

No guarantees

Private treatment is not a total guarantee of satisfaction either. Robert suffered from diabetes and when he injured an ankle the wound failed to respond to treatment and eventually turned gan-grenous. Care in a private clinic failed to restore his health, and it became necessary for the affected leg to be removed before his entire system was infected. The day after this was done, a funeral director appeared at the door of his private room and presented a bill to his wife.

'I was still in a state of shock,' she explained. 'I did not want any further hassle with the worry about Bob and all the to-ing and fro-ing between home and hospital. So I wrote out a cheque. He said it was to cover disposal of the limb they had removed because it had been taken to the crematorium as the clinic did not have facilities to dispose of it. The medical insurance did not cover it, he pointed out. I have since asked around and nobody seems to think what happened was quite right. I wish I had been a little less ready to part with the €540 demanded.' Inquiries were still going ahead some months later though it does not appear that this is common practice. But be careful.

Dentistry

One area where paying is the common way of securing a release from pain is dentistry. Many good dentists abound among the polyglot communities along the Spanish coast, and the best way of getting the care you want is to ask around and then be treated by a dentist that someone who has been there before you recommends. That applies to the cost as well as the level of competence, for dental care is not cheap. Private insurance is available to cover dental and orthodontic costs, and it is a matter of choice for individuals as to what level of cover and regularity of inspection their teeth require.

Residential care

It is recommended by British consular officials that people should make provision for when one partner or the other dies or they reach a stage where they have no way of looking after themselves.

The Spanish system is not as good in this respect as in the UK on picking up people who are not capable of looking after themselves. The residential or nursing home idea is in its infancy in Spain and places are not as readily available as in the UK.

Should a place become necessary and one be found in Spain, the chances are that the person in need will have to check into what is a totally Spanish environment which may not be completely to the liking of an ageing Briton. Facilities generally are not up to the UK standard and, in any case, it will mean having to pay and that could over-stretch the pension available.

As time goes on, it may be necessary for older people to return to the UK while they are still fit enough, so that either the family can care for them or they can become part of the UK scheme of things again before it is too late to make proper provision. If someone has lived in Spain for 20 years or so and then, when a partner dies or illness strikes, returns to the UK, it may be some time (perhaps six months or more) before they have re-established their UK residence and entitlement to various benefits.

Nursing care

In many cases, nursing care is only now coming in as far as the Spanish health service is concerned. *Practicantes*, comparable to our district nurses, used to be available in the community, but their training was limited and consisted mainly of administering injections. More recently, they have been replaced by *auxiliares de enfermería* (auxiliary nurses or care assistants). The chief reason for the increased need now for help in caring for frail older people is that families are much smaller now than formerly, when there was always at least one member of the family available to help.

Another area of interest to the elderly, that is becoming better known in Spain in recent years, concerns mobility. The range of wheelchairs, mobility scooters, baths and stair lifts that have become well known in the UK are making an appearance among the expatriate population, too. Hiring is available in some places and prices tend to be below UK levels.

They are, however, not as likely to be needed as often along the Mediterranean coast as they would be in the UK. The reason is the climate. This has a markedly beneficial effect on many who suffer from arthritic or rheumatic ailments. Each autumn, long-stay visitors who either move into their own holiday homes or make the most of hotel offers for those who can remain out of the fog and frost of northern Europe until Easter-time, arrive with their sticks and pills. Within a few weeks, or even days, it is surprising how many feel a relief from the aches in their joints and become much more sprightly.

It has been known for crutches and even wheelchairs to be left behind in bars or restaurants after a hearty night out, the refreshed foreigners obviously forgetting that they needed such assistance on the way there.

Catarrh sufferers seem to have varied responses to the milder atmosphere with some finding a clogged nose something soon forgotten while others need to continue with their medication in order to breathe easily. There does generally seem to be a lower incidence of the regular round of colds and 'flu' that affect folk influenced by the cold and damp winter air of higher latitudes, but of course this will be influenced by which part of Spain you live in.

One condition that is almost endemic in parts of Spain is gallstones. Due to the high level of calcium in the water in areas where the supply is drawn from within the limestone rock, many locals suffer from a build-up of stones in their internal organs. It does not appear to be a particular problem among the expatriate community, however, probably because they do not drink a great quantity of water from straight out of the tap, preferring to use one or other of the many bottled varieties available. Or maybe it takes a lifetime of imbibing water from local wells and reservoirs for the chalk build-up to occur. Often, today, the treatment is by laser rather than the surgeon's knife – but this won't be suitable for all patients, unfortunately.

13 Security

The attitude to criminals

Bill had just finished putting a coat of paint on the lounge ceiling and was on his way out to the car when he spotted the young man intently poking a length of welding rod down through the rubber on the passenger's window. Bill managed to catch the thief and hold him until the police arrived. They dumped him unceremoniously into their van and carted him away after warm handshakes and congratulations.

A couple of weeks later, one of the policemen informed Bill that the would-be thief's parents had lodged a complaint about the use of unnecessary force to make the arrest. 'Don't worry,' he added. 'Your name doesn't appear anywhere and we don't know who you are or where to find you.' And, grinning, he left.

Obviously there is crime in Spain, just as there is everywhere else. There is genuine resentment, however, at the continued use of the 'Costa del Crime' tag, which was coined after a handful of villains took up residence on the Costa del Sol a quarter of a century ago, and which is still employed by sub-editors too lazy to come up with their own headline. All those grills on the windows are not there traditionally just for decoration, and the fact that they have formed part of the scene for many years hints at a less than totally secure past. With holidaymakers being, perhaps, less careful with belongings than they would be at home, thefts occur on a regular basis.

Direct helpline

Loss through burglary will not be recompensed by insurance companies unless there is a police report to back up the claim, and the same goes for the theft of a purse or handbag. This can involve considerable time and effort, but there is a way of short-circuiting some of the paperwork and getting things moving more quickly. This is to use the helpline which has been set up by the National Police to speed up the whole process and save them valuable time as well. You can report anything which you feel they ought to know about – and a robbery or break-in definitely comes under this heading.

The number to ring is **902 102 112** or they can be contacted by email on www.policia.es. Officers are on hand who speak English, German, French and Italian as well as Spanish who will fill in the appropriate form for you. You have to sign it, of course, but this can be done at any police station throughout Spain which you nominate where the document will be forwarded When you get there, the benefit is that you by-pass the queue and go straight in and sign because there is nothing more for you to do.

There is also an emergency number – **112** – which is manned 24 hours a day by staff speaking the more common foreign languages. Tell them which service you require, and they arrange everything for you, acting as interpreter so that your local fire brigade or ambulance personnel do not have the additional problem of understanding what a non-Spanish speaker is trying to tell them.

Not all incidents – especially robberies – are treated seriously by police, however. Part of the reason is that too many tourists report the theft of valuables – and especially cash – in what are clearly suspicious circumstances. Each individual case might be considered genuine in isolation, but when so many are so similar, police soon recognise the trend. It is a sad fact that many visitors try and cash in on their holiday insurance for, with £200 being the limit for a cash claim, that is most often what is reported as having been stolen. Of course, a report from the police has to accompany the claim on the return home and, so, the police waste their time. This does little to encourage them to help those who fall victim to genuine attacks and tends to rebound on all foreigners whenever they seek police help.

Things to watch

So how safe are you in Spain? The answer is that in most areas you are at least as safe as you would be in the UK. There are places and times of day when it is not too clever to be about. But that applies in all countries. A little thought can prevent most problems. However, there are things to watch for.

Gypsies selling tablecloths still visit some areas and, while they may be just what they appear, they could be the advance guard on the lookout for others who will follow. If they call, keep an eye open. Some urbanisations have a system whereby anyone seeing gypsies around, blows a whistle to alert the neighbourhood.

There are lots of bag snatchings and car robberies in airport and supermarket car parks.

You may also receive a visit from a man armed with a clipboard who claims to be checking your gas installations. If you do, ask for his credentials and make sure they are those of someone from the company who supplies your gas. If in any doubt, ring the company that replenishes your gas bottles; a genuine man will not mind waiting while you do this and a dodgy one will disappear. These bogus gasmen always find a split in the rubber hose connecting your bottle to the house (he will make one himself with a Stanley knife if there isn't one) and charge anything he thinks you'll stand for the few coppers worth of tubing with which he replaces it. He may try and sell you a new valve to fit the top of the bottle as well. This is likely to have come from the last place he called at while yours will be sold on to the next house he visits.

Don't let him in until you have checked. The genuine inspections take place every five years, are for your safety, and you will receive a certificate to say all is well. If you have a certificate, do not let anyone else tamper with your fittings while it is current.

One dodge that is perpetrated across the Continent is used on roads outside airports and in car parks. It consists of someone pointing out that your car has a puncture (which they probably caused in the first place) and, while they are helping change the wheel, an accomplice makes the most of your distraction to help themselves to a handbag, radio or other valuables from the car. By the time you notice the loss, you have thanked them for their help and they are on their way.

The police

In Spain, the structure of the police force is vastly different from that to which anyone from Britain is accustomed. In effect, it is a three-pronged trident rather than a single-pointed spear. The objective is the same, however – to stop the selfish and the violent from disrupting their neighbours from going about their lawful occasions.

It is confusing for the foreigner at first, with policemen coming in the three distinct uniforms of dark blue, an even darker blue that is almost black and drab green. And they wear different hats and belts and carry various weapons from batons, handcuffs and pistols to machine guns.

Guardia Civil

Most impressive are the members of the *Guardia Civil*, whose duties include manning the frontiers of the realm and the responsibility for keeping order among the mounting millions driving on the country's major roads. They are more remote from the populace than the other two branches of the police in that they live barrack-style in segregated accommodation and maintain a military appearance. Indeed, there was a time not long ago when, under General Franco, it was felt that they were not so much there to make certain that the civilian population was safe, as to keep those set in authority well out of harm's way should anyone decide it was time for an unauthorised change in the status quo. In many parts of the country, members of the *Guardia Civil* were very unpopular due to the power they had, and the way they used it under Franco.

Their role, however, has moved into the area of the protection of civilians' rights, their well-armed state enabling them to deal on even terms with those who seek to impose their will through terrorism.

They have, for example, proved an effective thorn in the side of ETA (the Basque separatist group, analogous perhaps to the IRA). Despite knowing this, it can still be very disconcerting for an Englishman to be confronted on a remote lakeside or river bank by a pair of them carrying enough firepower to stop a boatload of drug smugglers who just want to look at his fishing licence. That, however, is part of their duties for theirs is the onus of keeping peace in the countryside where many a hunter is, of course, well armed.

It is worth noting that they have the right to confiscate not only rods and reels but guns or vehicles which are being used illegally.

Like the National police – who are in dark blue uniforms which are to all intents and purposes black – a growing part of their work involves tracking drugs and those who supply them. With land frontiers now wide open and hashish available virtually like chocolate just across the Mediterranean in Morocco, keeping all manner of drugs off the streets is a major headache. And the *Guardia* also provide the Customs officers who check passports and protect borders.

National police

The Corps of *Policia National* most closely resemble their British counterparts, especially since they changed to their present uniforms from brown ones in the Nineties. They also provide the plain-clothes men who do the under-cover work associated with the detective branch in the UK.

The extra effort involved in curtailing drug abuse has left them – like almost every police force around the world – seriously undermanned. Much of the work of the National Police, however, is concerned with documentation, for they are in charge of provision of *residencias* and all the other pieces of paper required by foreign residents, as well as the issue of personal identity cards – which every Spaniard has to carry – and passports for those in their district.

The chain of command is straightforward, with each office answerable to a local headquarters, normally in the capital of the province. In the larger regions, several provinces may be combined in one large unit. All the forces in Spain are part of such a similar network, and all of them come under the aegis of the Ministry of the Interior in Madrid.

Anything affecting the security of the public is their concern whether it be thefts resulting from break-ins from houses and vehicles or muggings, bank hold-ups, murders and other violent criminal activity. Each force is ostensibly responsible for its own area, but cover is always available from neighbouring stations when more manpower is required.

A *comisario* – roughly equivalent to a British superintendent – is the man in charge of each unit, and he answers to a chief superintendent while an officer corresponding to an assistant chief constable holds the reins in each province with his chief in the regional head-quarters. Under the *comisario* are the *policías* (the constables) whose next step up the command ladder is to *suboficial* (relative to a corporal in the army) and then *sub-inspector* (sergeant). *Inspector* is the first commissioned rank, which has the station commander above that.

As with the *Guardia Civil*, members of the National force tend to work in parts of the country well away from their home areas, though the insistence on the localised language being used has made it virtually impossible for recruits from outside Cataluña, for instance, to move there. Vacancies are, however, filled by men from other places, often those with seniority elsewhere. To move to a favoured spot such as one of the *costas*, a man may well have had to put in 15 years before his request for a transfer on the central list in Madrid is lucky. A man from the north, for instance, could be told his application for a move to Andalucía is possible as there is a vacancy in Córdoba. He can either take the offer or wait and hope that the move to the coast he really wanted will come along.

Local police

Local recruitment is obviously the case with the Local Police, the men in blue who are most commonly seen on the streets. These

Policías Locales are the ones who tighten the often unnoticed yet vital nuts and bolts which allow the wheels of law enforcement to function. They are primarily concerned with the more mundane facets of life ... things such as quarrels between neighbours, the maltreatment of animals or children, and parking problems on market day.

Yet their main purpose is much the same as that of their perhaps more romantic colleagues – the security of the municipality, the maintenance of peace which allows ordinary folk to go about their daily lives unmolested. Paid for by the local town hall, they make sure that things go smoothly in the district. They escort the mayor and his or her councillors and other dignitaries when protocol or necessity demands; they make sure public meetings are conducted in an orderly fashion; they man the crossings when children go to school; and deal with the many *denuncias* that follow minor traffic accidents or arguments over dogs (more of which later).

That they have local knowledge is essential if the men on duty are to have answers to the many relatively trivial questions with which they are confronted but which are important to the person asking.

Each local force operates within its own municipal boundaries and is a unique corps, though they all come under the overall cover of the regional government. Despite wearing the same uniform, they are often distinct in character for the problems of an inland farming community, for instance, are quite different from those that have to be dealt with in a bustling, tourist spot often inundated with people from a host of nationalities rarely seen in the remoter hinterland. There is, though, a willingness to give cross-border aid.

With three shifts a day to man, they also seldom have enough men to deal with the workload, though many now have motorcycle patrols, and some even have mounted sections to help cover their territory. They also work closely with the *vigilancias* who are not police at all though they do wear police-style outfits. These are private guards employed on estates and urbanisations and represent security firms.

Of course, the degree of co-operation among all these agencies depends on the relationships between the individuals concerned in each area, but it is unusual not to find them sharing information and giving backing whenever it is required.

Denuncias

The system whereby the Spaniard sorts out a dispute with his neighbour or seeks recompense from someone who has damaged his car is to make a *denuncia* against them – in fact, to denounce them to the police. It sounds like a good idea as, with a means of reconciling differences so easily to hand, it should stop anyone feeling the need to resort to violence, at least in theory. If you have a grievance, you write the details down at the local police station (in Spanish, and there are interpreters to help in many of the larger municipalities). The person complained against is then visited by the police and, if the matter cannot be resolved by their intervention, the issue is put before a judge in a lower court when the law's decision will be handed down.

The normal Spanish reaction to any *denuncia* made against them is to make an immediate counter accusation against the plaintiff. This means that if the parties cannot agree, the judge will hear of the incident from two sides and then decide.

As an example, in return for asking a man working next door to stop bashing some metal about unnecessarily and making so much racket, Alan was hit with a piece of steel and had to have several stitches in an ear. Armed with the medical evidence, he made a *denuncia* against the perpetrator to ensure there was no recurrence. He turned up at court a few weeks later, and the culprit was duly given a sentence of house arrest for a month and ordered to pay damages.

Then Alan was asked how he pleaded to the charge against him. This was the first he knew of any complaint, but it transpired that the man who had hit him had counter claimed that he had only hit the Englishman because he had hit his 11-year-old son. And the

Spaniard's wife told the court her son had returned home bruised and crying. Alan told the court that he could remember seeing the lad there but had not even spoken to him and certainly had not struck him. However, he was given a week's house arrest himself. He was assured that as it was deemed only a misdemeanour, the sentence would not be on any criminal record, for he did not want to be branded as having assaulted a minor.

So, each day, he was visited at a random hour by the local police to ensure he did not leave his home for the required period, just as his attacker was.

Like anyone else charged with an offence, either by a *denuncia* or by the police, Alan could have appealed the decision of the local court to the provincial court. This would have involved employing a solicitor as nobody can approach the higher court without benefit of counsel. Any such appeal also requires the posting of a bond which measure is to ensure that no one takes such a step frivolously. Unless things are pretty desperate, it pays to leave *denuncias* to the locals.

Bad debts

Anyone who conducts any sort of business transaction – and that can include working, or selling or purchasing a house, a car or furniture – can come across the bad debt scene. Sadly, much of it is liable to involve fellow expatriates who convince themselves that honesty and decency are things that can be dispensed with once they have crossed the Channel.

Sometimes you can feel sympathy for the debtors. They have given their ideas a try, put their own savings and all their effort into a venture, then sunk under the pressure of too little capital and too small an income chasing too many outgoings. This sympathy is naturally greater for those who acknowledge what has happened and offer to pay over a protracted period than it is for those who simply disappear to be heard of from Santo Domingo or Singapore.

Another case involved a British 'businessman' who tore up a bill with which he was presented and announced that, as it was under the limit below which a debt could not be processed through the courts there was nothing anyone could do. In the short term, he was correct but, once word went round, his company's turnover tumbled until the takings terminated and he wound up selling time-share.

However, if it is a 'processable' debt and the person keen on not paying is still in Spain, you have a fair chance of getting your money back through the courts. In many cases the advice about having expert guidance is sound. You can go along and make a *denuncia* on your own, but any such action can drag on for years. Lawyers who have helped others pass this way can more than earn their fee for they will know all about the dreaded embargo system. This is a legal search for funds to meet bad debts which can freeze bank accounts and stop you selling your property. It can be called down by a judge in favour of an individual as well as the government or council out to recover unpaid taxes.

Of course, going to the law like this takes time, sometimes an awful lot of it. If the debt comes in the form of a rubber cheque, though, other options are open which can speed up the whole problem of gaining what is rightfully yours. Once a cheque has been returned because insufficient funds are in the account to cover it, the holder has a choice of action.

Firstly, they can ask the bank on which the offending paper is drawn to tell them how much is, in fact, in the account. This the bank is obliged to do by law. For instance, if the cheque is for €500 and you discover that the account has €300 in it, you can take that – all of it – have the cheque annotated, and return at any time within the six months from the date it was made out during which period it is valid, and take out the remainder, or anything else that is in there towards the outstanding amount of €200.

Should the account holder get coy and not put any more in, you can still denounce them before the end of the six-month period or take the cheque along to a *Notario* and claim *Acta de Reclamation de Pago*, which will also put the cheque into the court process. But, at least, you will have recovered some money.

Armed collectors

There is, however, a second and much more satisfactory method of calling down the wrath of the law on any defaulter. The holder of a bouncing cheque can take it along to the local *Guardia Civil* whose duty it then becomes to recover the money. It is one thing to have a person standing at the door waving a dud cheque trying to persuade you to part with the readies, but an entirely different prospect when a couple of gun-toting men in uniform come to present it.

Their powers of recovery are prompt, too. Should they feel so inclined they can stipulate that the money be handed to them in a matter of hours ... or the defaulter must go to jail until the debt is paid. Issuing a false cheque is, you see, a criminal offence in Spain and they can call down the full weight of the law of the land to force anyone to hand over whatever amount is written on the cheque. Another advantage is that the process is relatively simple and, as you have the *Guardia* acting for you, legal representation is not necessary.

One case in point concerned a cheque for 80,000 pesetas which was written in good faith but, before it was presented, a standing order took the account below that figure. The result was that the cheque bounced. The person who had received the cheque had the bank stamp it to prove there were insufficient funds in the account to cover the amount, and went straight to the *Guardia Civil*. They duly rolled up at the account holder's home at 11am to be told that it was purely an oversight and that things would be put straight at once. 'In that case,' they said, 'we expect the money before 3 o'clock'.

Feeling slightly aggrieved that he had not been given the opportunity to explain the situation and pay without their intervention, he arrived within a couple of hours with the money – all 80,000 coins in bags to cover the amount. The point was, of course, that the person collecting the cash had to count it to the satisfaction of the *Guardia* before he could sign for it! The message got through very clearly that it is far better to sort these things out without recourse to the law if you can and not make them spend their time acting as debt collectors unless it really is necessary.

14 Common complaints

Noisy motor bikes

Colin and Barbara had driven from the coast up into the mountains, passed through the village marked on the map and continued upwards again on a suspension and tyre-ruining track until even that petered out. But it had been worth it, they felt, as they followed the gravel trail on foot among the cork oaks and umbrella pines. A cluster of white-walled houses clung to a distant mountain face, and lonely farms were dotted in such incongruous places that it was impossible to trace any means of access to them. A family of wild pigs moved along the hillside across the valley, and though no deer were spotted it was likely that deer were watching them. It was idyllic.

Then they heard the distant din, and it grew louder. Into sight round a bend came a yellow motor scooter which had no discernible exhaust system. The local postman waved as he blasted his way passed them on his rural round and they *buenos diased* him back. What a wonderful job he had … a 20-kilometre circuit on rustic trails through woods and mountains to deliver the mail to remote homesteads. However, with that racket, he would see no wildlife, no self-respecting animals or birds at any rate.

And this one man and his machine epitomised much of what constitutes the two most frequently listed complaints about living in Spain. Noise for one, and the postal service, that most vilified of Spanish institutions, the *Correos*, for the other.

Those who do not know Spain well, or have not been there at all, imagine the sound of the country to consist of the throb of flamenco guitars and the clack of castanets. Those who know it better realise the most pervasive sounds are the cacophony of high-revving, unsilenced engines and the barking of dogs. Once in a while some enterprising police department organises a blitz and rounds up a few dozen – or even hundreds – of buzzing motor bikes which are only returned to their owners when some sort of exhaust system has been fitted. Little engines do not provide the macho speed or sound required, however, and the baffles are soon removed so that the bored-out cylinder can do its worst once more.

Thirty years ago there were more mules and donkeys than cars in rural Spain, and that was everywhere outside the major cities. Car ownership was confined to the wealthy and privileged, much as it was in England before the Second World War. The man who had made a few pesetas impressed his neighbours by arriving at the bar on a moped and, naturally, he wanted everybody to know. So a healthy blast from the back end was nothing to try and muffle. His grandchildren are part of the first generation who have been able to go to school on motorised wheels. Is it any wonder they are not overly concerned about how much nuisance their passing causes anyone?

The truth is that the locals do not seem to notice noise anything like as much as do their foreign neighbours, so conversation-stopping mopeds are something to which the expatriate may simply have to adjust whatever legislation is enacted.

Barking dogs

The same applies to dogs. Did you know that people going aloft into the silent world of hot-air balloons find the sound that reaches them most clearly as they float across the countryside is that of dogs barking? Until relatively recently, pets were not regarded with the same reverence with which they are cherished in many Western countries and earned their keep by working with livestock, keeping down rodents or guarding premises. It is not unnatural, therefore, that many Spanish dogs still see their purpose in life as being to protect their territory. As this largely consists of barking as loudly as possible at anything and everything passing by, with owners making little or no attempt to quell their enthusiasm, it is not surprising that man's best friend should spend his time making all and sundry aware that he is doing his job. They are mostly intelligent, though, and in relatively short order a little stern friendship usually makes things tolerable. Should that fail there is always the local police whose duty it is to prevent undue interference with people's sleep.

The other oft-heard complaint about dogs is that the evidence of their passing is all too evident in some places. Despite fines being imposed for owners of dogs which foul footpaths, free collection bags being made available and even dog toilets being provided in parks, there are clearly those who take no notice. Generally, the nuisance is not as bad as it was, but for those who have to play hopscotch when they would simply like to walk along the pavement it is irritating to find there is such a nuisance at all. It seems that canine residue is something folk have to endure whether they live in Torremolinos or Torquay, Barcelona or Bournemouth.

If you own a dog and live in a rural area where there are sheep, be sure it does not attack any. This act would be considered very serious and could have grave consequences for both owner and dog.

The postal service

If only it were as easy to find a solution to the *Correos*. People whose livelihoods involve postal deliveries have been known to return to the land from which they came in sheer frustration. Although the problems do vary from one area to another, everybody encounters delays to both incoming and outgoing mail. Many people who have become accustomed to two visits a day from the post-person have to get used to the idea that letters tend to arrive on more like a twice-weekly basis.

Charles, for instance, had found that the cost of having his photographs developed at the local camera shop was about double what he paid if he used the postal-print service available in the UK. A couple of times it worked all right. His next film vanished, or so it seemed. After a month and, with a holiday looming and wanting to take the prints with him, he went to the nearest sorting office. His luck was in, for the person he found behind the counter was the man who had been on the round which included his house until he had been promoted the year before. Explaining the position, Charlie was ushered into a back office and shown a scree slope composed of thousands of envelopes spilling down the rear wall. He knew his pictures would be in a green envelope so he delved and, on the second go, found the one with his name on. 'How long might my pictures have remained buried under that lot?' he wondered.

The word for a letter box is *buzón*, and the same name or the term *apartado de correos* is given to rows of little hutches with locked doors which line a wall in all main post offices. They can be hired and once you own a key, all your mail is left in your *apartado* for collection. If you live on an irregular postal route or want items as soon as they arrive, they do mean you do not have to wait until they are brought to the house. There is normally a waiting list, however.

Ruth had waited ages for the delivery of a parcel containing jewellery she had bought over the phone from a TV shopping channel. She filled in the appropriate form to complain at the local post office. 'I know not to use the postal service unless necessary', she said. 'That's why I order by telephone nowadays and contact my friends by email, but some things simply have to be delivered. How long am I supposed to wait?'

The letter of apology she received from the person in charge of postal services for the area pointed out that, with staff shortages and an increasing population, they did indeed, have problems. They went on to add that with new personnel they had the disadvantage that some of them did not know where all the streets were on their route, let alone the houses.

'I got my package in the end,' Ruth said, 'but what I was told, in effect, was that I must not expect things to improve.'

The building boom really has made the postal problem worse, for in several rapidly-growing coastal areas the person on the scooter has twice as many houses to call on compared with a few years before.

One declared that he could not carry all the post for that district on his bike any more, so they had to split up the load enabling him to deliver to part of the round only each day. The result was a delivery no more than twice a week, unless there was a heavier load than normal in which case some would only see him once.

Percy knew about delays and determined to see everyone got his cards on time a couple of Christmases ago. He congratulated himself as the whole of his card list was ticked off and every envelope stamped and posted by the end of November. Nobody got a greeting from him until the middle of January, however, for they were all franked out of the main sorting office on 2nd January. 'Whatever happened to December?' he asked.

Many parcels addressed to expatriates simply never arrive. There is a feeling that there must be an aircraft hangar-sized building somewhere full of undelivered items. A complete manuscript of this book, winging its way back from editor to author, is probably one of them, for it simply vanished *en route*! However, there is always the exception and when things click, two days may see letters from the UK with the Spanish recipient. In the reverse direction the mail can work efficiently, too. Items cleared at midday on, say, Tuesday sometimes arrive through a UK letterbox first post on Thursday. In Málaga, strangely, it seems usually to be letters sent on a Tuesday that make the best time.

Timekeeping

Another frequent 'moan' from those newly sorting out their lives in Spain concerns timekeeping and opening hours. What has to be overcome is the Anglo-Saxon expectation that things will be carried out, if not immediately, at least when someone says they will. The idea persists in many Spanish minds that if something is not fixed straight away you may find you can do without it and not have to put it right tomorrow, or indeed at all.

Builders give deadlines they fully intend to keep at the time. But they may give similar promises to several customers with the result that there is little possibility of anybody having a job completed according to schedule. They will all get done eventually, but there is a feeling that these foreigners make an inordinate amount of fuss about a few days – or weeks.

The resident also finds out what few holidaymakers need to know, and that is that an appointment for 11am is liable to mean any time before lunch. No insult is intended by the person who turns up late. For example, half an hour before the appointed time, they could have been having coffee when somebody they had been trying to catch happened to come into the bar. So the business that had been pending was done while they were both there. Once that was finished, they remembered the original appointment and hurried back full of apologies but nowhere near as concerned as your average Brit would be.

Many businesses do not open until 10am anyway and in those that do start earlier, like builders' merchants, the staff all knock off for breakfast from around 9.30 to 10. If the unsuspecting walk in during that break, they just have to wait awhile whether it is because nobody is about or the employees are sitting on a pile of bricks chatting. They will deal with whatever the problem is in their own good time.

Many larger stores and supermarkets do not observe the *siesta* too closely nowadays, but other businesses do. At anything from 1 to 2pm the doors are shut to be reopened for customers at 5 or 6pm with the busiest part of the day possibly being the hour before they close for the day at about 8 o'clock. That is unless it is a government office, official building or a bank. Then it will not be open again after lunchtime until the next morning. All official transactions, like getting *residencias* or paying bills or any sort of taxes, must be taken care of during the morning. Having to go through the paper chase of obtaining one in the first instance and then needing to begin all over again when renewing a *residencia* is itself a matter that causes moans.

Official paperwork

All this bureaucratic paperwork is another reason for complaint. Some of the irksome forms involved in things like car ownership, local taxes and other housing matters may be difficult to handle for the twin reasons that they are in a manner the foreigner is not used to and in a different language. Like timekeeping, however, this is how it is done, and things are not going to change to suit the way somebody is used to doing it in another country. You just have to get used to it.

Fiestas may also cause confusion. They are not always publicised too well, especially the local ones, because 'everybody' knows when they are – except foreigners, of course. It is a matter of planning to make sure there is no shortage of bread, milk and gas. And gas arriving by lorry in a dirty container rather than via a pipeline is another cause of complaint that becomes part of life's pattern over time.

Power cuts and water pressure

Power cuts in the electricity supply are not as frequent as they used to be in most areas. But they do happen during heavy storms or high winds in places and tend to be more of a nuisance factor than in the UK. Water may be subject to fluctuating pressure on a local level, and the amount of chlorine used to purify it is a cause for complaint in some localities. However, water quality is mainly better than in Britain in spite of the fear of drinking local water inherent in the British character. Hosepipe bans are rare in Spain despite the drier climate and the need for more garden watering in the hot months. When buying a home, ask around and look for water tanks on roofs which are a feature of some towns. They are a sure indication that the piped supply is not to be relied on. There have been some water shortages in recent dry years, and both residents and tourists have been asked not to waste water.

A complaint made about some Spanish dwellings is the lack of cupboard space. There is unlikely to be a special airing cupboard, for instance. With modern buildings it is less likely to prove troublesome, but in some older premises storage space for things like DIY tools, sports equipment and hobby materials may be at a premium. This is due in large part to the fact that until recently the average Spaniard had little in the way of material possessions to store, so no provision had to be made for them.

Time-share touts

One nuisance factor often referred to is an irritation that the tourist industry might well be said to have brought with it: time-share touts. The business of offering shared holiday ownership to people is based on some pretty intensive selling aimed at not letting potential customers be left unaware of what is available. To that end, any foreigner in an area where there are time-share resorts is liable to be targeted by enthusiastic sales people who will try and inveigle them into visiting the place. These 'uppers' are paid according to the number of clients they persuade to turn up to hear the sales pitch of the 'closers' at the complex, so they are obviously keen to keep up the average.

Most are affable enough and politely depart when told you are a resident and not therefore interested, nor indeed suitable as clients for the company they represent. Some, however, can be almost belligerent and holidaymakers will probably be familiar with their tactics. To a person domiciled in the locality even the nice approach can become tiresome after a time. When one local police force received numerous complaints from those being accosted, they did something about it by rounding up 39 sales persons operating on the streets in two days which restored order for a while, as well as bringing it to the attention of the companies involved that they might be overdoing things a little.

Some folk do take a trip to resorts in their area without letting on that they already live there. After all, it is a look around that fills in a damp afternoon and costs nothing. Others just get fed up with the approaches.

15 Going home

How many return?

In the third quarter of the Twentieth Century when Australia and Canada were the recipients of Britons heading for pastures new on a £10 assisted passage, some surprising statistics emerged. Half of those setting sail for Australia came back, and then half of those moved Down Under a second time … and stayed there.

Of course, they were mainly young people, many with children in tow, who were out to make a better life for themselves. The difference with those now making the move to Spain is that they are, in the main, older people who are looking not for work but rather to enjoy a well-earned retirement. The aim is the same, though – to enjoy a better lifestyle. Details of numbers returning to the United Kingdom are as difficult to obtain as are those concerning how many thousands are actually arriving in Iberia. The isolation factor is not the same either with a few hours in a plane being a totally different prospect – and consequently much cheaper – from weeks or even months in a ship or an airfare that for many was unthinkably expensive.

The percentages might well be similar, however. There is so much part-time retirement to Spain and so many living there without following all the legal procedures within the new framework of the European Union that no one will ever know.

It is, however, a fact that a considerable proportion of those who retire to the sun do return to their native shores. It is not that they have failed; it is simply that things do not always work out the way they had hoped. The previous chapter examined some of the more common complaints that irritate people arriving to live in Spain, and a combination of any of them may make some decide that they just do not want to put up with the annoyance any longer.

Most frequently the underlying reason for selling up and moving back is financial. That is almost always the case with the younger element who are looking to make their fortune in southern Europe. Spain can be a wonderful place to live but a difficult place to earn a living. But for the pensioner, changing circumstances – the loss of a husband or wife, ill health necessitating prolonged care and a move into residential accommodation – are often the prime causes that lead to financial constraints causing the forsaking of life in Spain to prove inevitable.

Family ties

The pull of family – especially grandchildren – is another unsettling factor which many find comes into the equation. And then there is the feeling of being foreign that some just cannot adjust to. This is often intertwined with the barrier of speaking the language which, for some people, is insurmountable. A relatively small problem over a tax bill from the town hall that was sent in error and was nothing to do with the recipient at all, for instance, can escalate through an unwillingness for anyone to help or show any interest into a loss of that comfortable understanding which is a major part of the feeling of acceptance in the community.

Break-ins destroy that sense of security and sanctity which are part of turning a house into a home wherever they occur. When they take place in a strange land where police methods differ, their effect is magnified. Thefts of purses and handbag snatches take away personal confidence from the victim whenever they happen, but it is harder to overcome the sense of being targeted by criminals in an unfamiliar environment. They are probably no more likely to be experienced in Spain than anywhere else, and the individual is safer there than in many parts of the United Kingdom if figures admitted by the Home Office are accepted. If they happen to pensioners on home territory there is, however, not the same desire to go somewhere else. For it is to the place in which we feel most safe that we instinctively turn when any kind of attack takes place. The belief that 'it is not safe here' is a major cause for anyone to go somewhere else wherever they are, and the British pensioner in Spain does not have the same roots to prevent them moving again.

Timing

Whatever the reason, timing is important for anyone returning to the UK. Tax considerations are probably more necessary than they are for those heading south, and there is always the relative prices of property to take into account. For anyone seeking to buy a home in Britain at the present time, for example, the disposal of their Spanish property is likely to leave them with a shortfall to take care of. Moving money from the euro to sterling is not something that has enhanced spending power recently either.

Plans do not always work out the way intended when people keep a house in the UK either. Take Mrs Watling's case. She was a widow who was comfortably off with a large family house in a pleasant English town. She had fallen in love with Spain though, and decided that her arthritis and general health – not to say her lifestyle in general – would be better there. She bought a villa and, for tax reasons, found it desirable not to remain a British resident but become officially domiciled in Spain. As a result – and with eventual death duties in mind as well – she made her English house over to her spinster daughter who had lived with her and who would continue to spend her time there while she furthered her career, though being a regular visitor to the Spanish coast.

The unforeseen happened, however. Her daughter died in an accident leaving her entire estate – including her mother's house – to the nephew of a friend, for whom she was godmother, and his wife. The fortunate couple had their own home in another part of the country and did not know their benefactor's mother. Consequently, they sold the house they did not want and left Mrs Watling, whose investments had suffered since the turn of the Millennium along with everyone else's, virtually stranded in Spain. When she decided she wanted to return to the UK, it was to a different existence and in the face of considerable further financial downturn.

For Mrs Angel, the decision to return was virtually made for her when her husband died. They had lived in a modest villa they jointly owned for several years, but with his death not only was her pension income reduced considerably but she was faced with the tax demand on the villa. The way this 7 per cent transfer tax works was pointed out back in Chapter 1, and suffice it here to say that the bill for transferring Mr Angel's half of the villa into her name was the equivalent of more than £6,000 which represented a large part of her capital. The result was that she sold her Spanish home and moved back to England to live with her daughter in the Midlands.

The Johnsons moved back after a few years in the sun, mainly for family reasons. He still owned the family business, which his sons ran, and he missed not being involved. And Mrs Johnson wanted to see her grandchildren grow up. They got a good price for their villa, found a reasonable bungalow near the family and fixed the date to move back. In true Spanish style, they sold all their furniture along with the villa, and determined to buy a car – which would be cheaper in Spain – to take their clothes and belongings with them.

Mr Johnson saw a right-hand-drive Jaguar advertised locally and paid cash to the Englishman who had decided to sell it after being in Spain a few months. Naturally, they told him why they wanted the car while he had a coffee with them when he delivered it. The day before they were due to head for the ferry, they packed all their treasured possessions into the car ready for an early start next morning. When they woke up however, the car had gone. The vendor of the Jag had obviously kept a spare key and, under cover of darkness, had pushed the car out of the driveway and then driven it away.

The Johnsons flew back to the UK with heavy hearts. The Jaguar, its precious contents – and the English 'previous' owner – have not been seen since.

Bereavement

Like Mrs Angel, many people who suffer bereavement in Spain, form a large proportion of those who return to the UK, as do the deceased. Funerals can be expensive in Spain and a lot of partners wish to ship the remains of their loved-one to somewhere that was special in their younger lives. The cost of sending a casket back to the UK can be horrifying, however. Crematoriums are a recent arrival on the Spanish scene, and this is a boon for many who do not want to have their relative stay permanently in Spain, for they have found that taking the ashes back in an urn is a better alternative. But, of course, not everyone wants to opt for cremation.

It is worth noting, however, that the British consular authorities cannot help out with repatriation of British citizens living or dead when their own funds are not sufficient for the purpose. While they stress that they appreciate individual circumstances, especially in bereavement, they cannot become involved in paying for travel to the UK. They can, and do, help in contacting family members or friends but are not there to send people home who become destitute or to assist with the repatriation of remains.

Whether you intend to return to the UK permanently or merely for a visit, you are likely to find that some of the bargain offers on airfares and ferry prices published in the UK are not so easy to obtain or, indeed, are impossible to find when going from Europe to the United Kingdom. But there are special airfares from various cities in Spain to the UK.

It is fair to say that with all the considerations of climate, lifestyle, economics and politics involved, most of those who decide to move their lives to Spain feel genuine sympathy for those who have to leave Iberia behind and return to the comparative greyness of their homeland. One ex-pat summed up this feeling in these words: 'Whenever I see a plane heading north I feel sorry for those on board. They are leaving Spain behind but I am lucky enough to be able to stay here'.

16 Useful addresses

NB These contact details are current at the time of publication but they do change from time to time: for up-to-date contact information go to
www.tourspain.co.uk
and click on the Useful Information section
then click on the button for British and Irish Consular and Diplomatic Representations in Spain.

If dialling from the UK, prefix telephone/fax numbers by 00 34.

The British Embassy

The British Embassy in Spain is in Madrid. You will need its services at least once every 10 years, when your passport has to be renewed.

C/Fernando el Santo, 16
28010 Madrid
Telephone: 91 700 82 00
91 524 97 00 (Consular); 91 524 97 27 (Visa)
Fax: 91 700 82 10
Email: enquiries.madrid@fco.gov.uk
Office hours (GMT) (Loc = +1hr):
Winter: 08.00–12.30 and 14.00–17.00
Summer: 07.30–14.00

Consulates

Madrid

British Consulate-General
Paseo de Recoletos, 7/9
28004 Madrid

Fax: 91 524 97 30
Office hours (GMT):
Winter: 06.30–13.30
Summer: 06.30–12.30

Alicante

British Consulate
Plaza Calvo Sotelo, 1–2
Apartado de Correos 564
03001 Alicante
Telephone: 96 521 60 22
Fax: 96 514 05 28
Email: enquiries.alicante@fco.gov.uk
Office hours (GMT):
Winter: 06.00–13.30
Summer: 06.00–12.30

Las Palmas (Canary Islands)

British Consulate
Edificio Cataluña
Calle Luis Morote, 6–3
35007 Las Palmas de Gran Canaria
(Postal address: PO Box 2020, 35080 Las Palmas de Gran Canaria)
Telephone: 928 26 25 08
Fax: 928 26 77 74
Email: laspalmasconsulate@ukinspain.com
Office hours (GMT):
Winter: 08.00–15.30
Summer: 07.00–14.30

Málaga

British Consulate
Edificio Eurocom
Calle Mauricio Moro Pareto, 2–2
29006 Málaga
Telephone: 952 35 23 00

Fax: 952 35 92 11
Email: postmaster@malaga.mail.fco.gov.uk
Office hours (GMT):
Winter: 07.00–14.30
Summer: 06.00–12.30

Santa Cruz de Tenerife

British Consulate (Canary Islands)
Plaza Weyler, 8–1
38003 Santa Cruz de Tenerife
Telephone: 922 28 68 63/922 28 66 53
Fax: 922 28 99 03
Email: tenerifeconsulate@ukinspain.com
Office hours (GMT):
Winter: 08.30–14.00
Summer: 08.00–13.30

Vigo

British Consulate
Plaza de Compostela, 23–61
(Apartado 49)
36201 Vigo
Telephone: 986 43 71 33
Fax: 986 43 71 33
Email: vigoconsulate@ukinspain.com
Office hours (GMT): 07.00–12.00

Barcelona

British Consulate-General
Edificio Torre de Barcelona
Avenida Diagonal, 477–13
08036 Barcelona
Telephone: 933 66 62 99 (6 lines)
Fax: 933 66 62 21
Email: bcon@cvberben,com
Website: www.ukinspain.com
Office hours (GMT):

April–June, September and October: 07.00–16.00
November to March: 08.00–7.00
July and August: 06.30–12.30

Bilbao

British Consulate-General
Alameda de Urquijo, 2–8
48008 Bilbao
Telephone: 94 415 76 00/94 415 77 11/94 415 77 22
Fax: 94 416 76 32
Airtech: 94 416 47 51
Email: bcgbilbo@readysoft.es
Office hours (GMT):
April–June, September and October: 07.00–16.00
November–March: 08.00–17.00
July and August: 06.30–12.30

Santander

British Consulate
Paseo de Pereda, 27
39004 Santander
Telephone: 942 22 00 00
Fax: 942 22 29 41
Email: mpineiro@nexo.es
Office hours (GMT):
April to mid-June, mid-September to October: 07.00–11.00 and
13.30–16.00
November to March: 08.00–12.00 and 14.30–17.30
Mid-June to mid-September: 06.00–12.30

Palma de Mallorca

British Consulate (Balearic Islands)
Plaza Mayor, 3D
07002 Palma de Mallorca.
Telephone: 971 71 24 45/971 71 20 85/971 71 60 48/971 71 85
01/971 71 26 96
Fax: 971 71 75 20

Email: consulate@palma.mail.fco.gov.uk
Office hours (GMT):
November to March: 07.00–14.30
April–June and September and October: 06.00–13.30
July and August: 06.00–12.30

Ibiza

British Vice-Consulate
Avenida Isidoro Macabich, 45–1
Apartado 307
07800 Ibiza
Telephone: 971 30 18 18/971 30 38 16/971 30 10 58
Fax: 971 30 19 72
Email: ibizacon@worldonline.es
Office hours (GMT):
November to March: 07.00–14.30
April, May, June, September and October: 06.00–13.30
July and August: 06.00–12.30

Menorca

Honorary British Vice-Consulate
Sa Casa Nova
Cami de Biniatap, 30
07720 Es Castell
Menorca
Telephone: 971 36 33 73
Fax: 971 35 46 90
Email: deborah@infotelecom.es

Andorra

Telephone and Fax: 376 83 98 40
Email: britcoand@mypic.ad

Department for Work and Pensions

Leaflets setting out your entitlement to benefits once you live out-side the United Kingdom are usually available from your local Social Services office. If they do not have them, they are obtainable from one of the most helpful branches of the Department for Work and Pensions. In fact, all inquiries regarding benefits which you may continue to receive once you leave the UK should be addressed to:
Department for Work and Pensions
The Pension Service
Tyneview Park
International Pension Centre
Newcastle-Upon-Tyne NE98 1BA
Tel: 0191 2183324 or 0191 2187580
Fax: 0191 2183315

Pets

Information on taking pets to Spain and, perhaps more importantly, on how to avoid problems should you wish to return them to the UK in the future, is available from the Department for Environment, Food and Rural Affairs on their PETS Helpline. This is available from 8.30 to 5pm, Monday to Friday on:
Tel: 0870 241 1710
Fax: 020 7904 6834
Website: www.defra.gov.uk/animalh/quarantine
Email: pets.helpline@defra.gsi.gov.uk

ABOUT AGE CONCERN ESPAÑA

The Spanish equivalent of the Age Concern everyone in the UK knows is correctly titled *Federación de Asociaciones de Age Concern España*. It is a federation of Age Concern Organisations in Spain, all of which are registered charities. They can be contacted at the following addresses:

Federación Age Concern España
Apartado 7
07180 Sta. Ponsa
Mallorca
email: federation@ageconcern-espana.org

A website is to be launched shortly.

Age Concern España can provide general information as well as specialist advice for people with more complex needs. It can also offer the following factsheets which are available free of charge (but a donation is always welcome) if you send a list of the ones you require and enclose a large self-addressed envelope:

1   Tele-Alarm
2   Breast cancer screening
3   Help with incontinence
4   Palma de Mallorca Social Services
5   Mallorca Social Services
6   Menorca Social Services
7   Ibiza Social Services
8   What to do in case of death
9   Personal check sheet
10 Glaucoma
11 Precautions against falls in the home
12 UK habitual residence test

In areas where there is a large population of English-speaking expatriates, there are local Age Concern Organisations. They can provide more detailed information about their own specific parts of the country. You can contact them at the addresses below:

Age Concern Costa Blanca Sur

Torreta III Centre
Calle Jaime Osto, 288–Polígono 2
03180 Torrevieja
Alicante

Age Concern Estepona y Manilva

Apartado 178
Sabinillas
29692 Manilva
Málaga

Age Concern Ibiza y Formentera

Apartado 370
07800 Ibiza

Age Concern Lanzarote

Apartado 287
35571 Macher
Lanzarote
Las Canarias

Age Concern Mallorca

Apartado 7
07180 Sta. Ponsa
Mallorca

Age Concern Menorca

Apartado 90
07720 Es Castell,
Menorca

ABOUT AGE CONCERN

Retiring to Spain is one of a wide range of publications produced by Age Concern England, the National Council on Ageing. Age Concern works on behalf of all older people and believes later life should be fulfilling and enjoyable. For too many this is impossible. As the leading charitable movement in the UK concerned with ageing and older people, Age Concern finds effective ways to change that situation.

Where possible, we enable older people to solve problems themselves, providing as much or as little support as they need. A network of local Age Concerns, supported by many thousands of volunteers, provides community-based services such as lunch clubs, day centres and home visiting.

Nationally, we take a lead role in campaigning, parliamentary work, policy analysis, research, specialist information and advice provision, and publishing. Innovative programmes promote healthier lifestyles and provide older people with opportunities to give the experience of a lifetime back to their communities.

Age Concern is dependent on donations, covenants and legacies.

Age Concern England
1268 London Road
London SW16 4ER
Tel: 020 8765 7200
Fax: 020 8765 7211
Website:
www.ageconcern.org.uk

Age Concern Scotland
13 Rose Street
Edinburgh EH2 3DT
Tel: 0131 220 3345
Fax: 0131 220 2779
Website:
www.ageconcernscotland.org.uk

Age Concern Cymru
4th Floor
1 Cathedral Road
Cardiff CF11 9SD
Tel: 029 2037 1566
Fax: 029 2039 9562
Website: www.accymru.org.uk

Age Concern Northern Ireland
3 Lower Crescent
Belfast BT7 1NR
Tel: 028 9024 5729
Fax: 028 9023 5497
Website:
www.ageconcernni.org

PUBLICATIONS FROM AGE CONCERN BOOKS

Your Rights: A guide to money benefits for older people

Sally West

A highly acclaimed annual guide to the State benefits available to older people. It contains current information on Income Support, Housing Benefit and retirement pensions, among other matters, and provides advice on how to claim.

For more information, please telephone 0870 44 22 120

Better Health in Retirement

Dr Anne Roberts

Retirement can be a time of great activity – and many people wonder how they found time to work. It can also be a time when people face greater health difficulties. It is important, therefore, that we continue to look after our health – or break the bad habits that we have built up over the years – so that we can look forward to a long and healthy retirement. Topics covered include:

- developing a healthy lifestyle
- health checks and screening
- common illnesses in later life
- using the health service
- help for older carers

£6.99 0-86242-251-5

How to be a Silver Surfer: A beginner's guide to the internet 2nd Edition

Emma Aldridge

This bestselling guide has been completely revised and updated, with new chapters on shopping, banking, family trees and gardening, all using the Internet. It is a companion guide for people who are new to the Internet and a little apprehensive about what to do. Using simple step-by-step explanations, it will 'hand-hold' readers through the most important tasks when first using the Internet. Topics include searching the web, sending an email and saving a favourite web page for future reference.

Aimed at the over 50s, the emphasis is on using the Internet as a tool to enrich existing interests, such as travel, fishing, aromatherapy, cooking and furniture restoration, and as a recreational activity in itself, including on-line bridge, emailing family and friends, and chat sites. It can also ensure you don't miss out on good deals and last minute bargains.

£5.99 0-86242-379-1

If you would like to order any of these titles, please write to the address below, enclosing a cheque or money order for the appropriate amount (plus £1.99 p&p for one book; for additional books, please add 75p per book up to a maximum of £7.50) made payable to Age Concern England. Credit card orders may be made on 0870 44 22 120. Books can also be ordered online at www.ageconcern.org.uk/shop

Age Concern Books
Units 5 and 6, Industrial Estate
Brecon
Powys LD3 8LA

Bulk order discounts

Age Concern Books is pleased to offer a discount on orders totalling 50 or more copies of the same title. For details, please contact Age Concern Books on Tel: 0870 44 22 120.

Customised editions

Age Concern Books is pleased to offer a free 'customisation' service for anyone wishing to purchase 500 or more copies of the title. This gives you the option to have a unique front cover design featuring your organisation's logo and corporate colours, or adding your logo to the current cover design. You can also insert an additional four pages of text for a small additional fee. Existing clients include many of the biggest names in British industry, retailing and finance, the Trades Union Movement, educational establishments, the statutory and voluntary sectors, and welfare associations. For full details, please contact Sue Henning, Age Concern Books, Astral House, 1268 London Road, London SW16 4ER. Fax: 020 8765 7211. Email: hennings@ace.org.uk

Visit our Website at www.ageconcern.org.uk/shop

Age Concern Information Line/ Factsheets subscription

Age Concern produces 44 comprehensive factsheets designed to answer many of the questions older people (or those advising them) may have. Topics covered include money and benefits, health, community care, leisure and education, and housing. For up to five free factsheets, telephone 0800 00 99 66 (7am-7pm, seven days a week, every day of the year). Alternatively you may prefer to write to Age Concern, FREEPOST (SWB 30375), ASHBURTON, Devon TQ13 7ZZ.

For professionals working with older people, the factsheets are available on an annual subscription service, which includes updates throughout the year. For further details and costs of the subscription, please write to Age Concern England at the above Freepost address.

INDEX

We hope that this publication has been useful to you. If so, we would very much like to hear from you. Alternatively, if you feel that we could add or change anything, then please write and tell us, using the following Freepost address: Age Concern, FREEPOST CN1 794, London SW16 4BR